# 'Tis So Sweet to Trust in Jesus

A 40-DAY JOURNEY TO THE CROSS
THROUGH THE WORDS OF CHRIST

*This study belongs to:*

_____

_____

THE DAILY GRACE CO.®

*'Tis So Sweet to Trust in Jesus: A 40-Day Journey to the Cross Through the Words of Christ*
Copyright © 2025 by The Daily Grace Co.®
Spring, Texas. All rights reserved.

Unless otherwise noted, all Scripture quotations are taken from the Christian Standard Bible®, Copyright © 2020 by Holman Bible Publishers. Used by permission. Christian Standard Bible® and CSB® are federally registered trademarks of Holman Bible Publishers.

Scripture quotations marked NIV are taken from the Holy Bible, New International Version®, NIV®. Copyright © 1973, 1978, 1984, 2011 by Biblica, Inc.® Used by permission of Zondervan. All rights reserved worldwide. www.zondervan.com. The "NIV" and "New International Version" are trademarks registered in the United States Patent and Trademark Office by Biblica, Inc.®

The extra on pages 20–21 is from *40 Days with Jesus: A Study on the Life of Christ*. Copyright © 2021 by the Daily Grace Co.® Learn more about this resource on page 218.

Supplemental material: pages 6–15, 214–215. Copyright © 2019 by The Daily Grace Co.®

The Daily Grace Co.® exists to equip disciples to know and love God and His Word by creating beautiful, theologically rich, and accessible resources so that God may be glorified and the gospel made known.

Designed in the United States of America and printed in China.

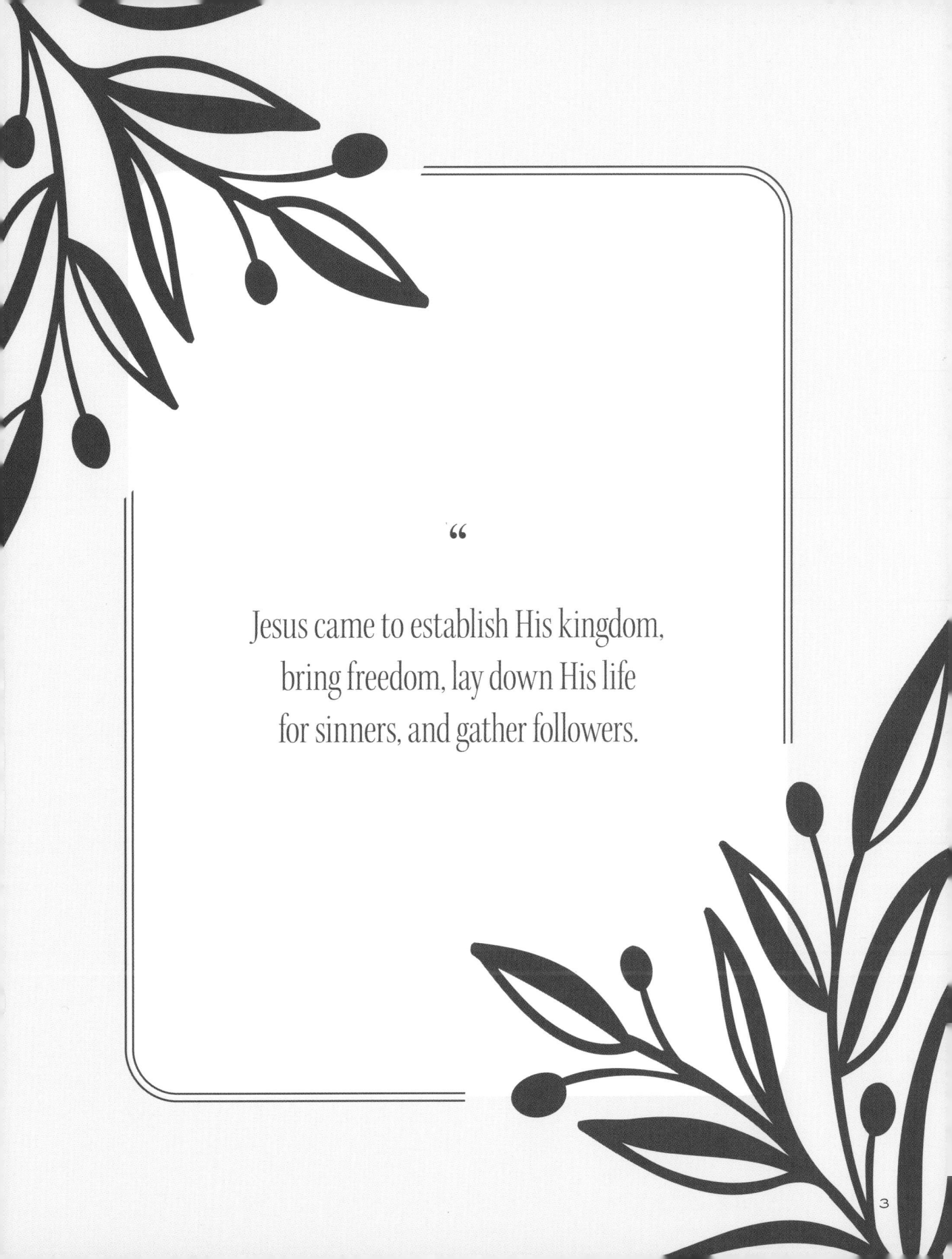

"

Jesus came to establish His kingdom,
bring freedom, lay down His life
for sinners, and gather followers.

# In This Study

## introduction

Study Suggestions ............................................. 6
How to Study the Bible ..................................... 8
The Attributes of God ..................................... 10
Timeline of Scripture ...................................... 12

## Before You Start

Metanarrative of Scripture ........................ 14
How to Use This Study .............................. 16
Lent Schedule ............................................. 20

## week one

Week 1 Memory Verse + Introduction .... 25
Day 1: Good News That
         Demands a Response ................... 27
Day 2: Good News for the Poor ............. 31

## Words about What Jesus Came to Do

Day 3: The Greatest Demonstration
        of God's Love ................................. 35
Day 4: Follow Me ...................................... 39
Week 1 Conclusion .................................... 42

## week two

Week 2 Memory Verse + Introduction .... 45
Day 5: The Bread of Life ........................... 47
Day 6: The Light of the World ................ 51
Day 7: The Gate and the
        Good Shepherd .............................. 55

## Jesus's "I Am" Statements

Day 8: The Resurrection and the Life .... 59
Day 9: The Way, the Truth,
        and the Life .................................... 63
Day 10: The True Vine ............................... 67
Week 2 Conclusion .................................... 70

## week three

Week 3 Memory Verse + Introduction .... 73
Day 11: The Beatitudes ............................. 75
Day 12: I Will Give You Rest .................... 79
Day 13: Jesus and Children ..................... 83
Day 14: A House of Prayer ....................... 87

## Words That Reveal Jesus's Heart

Day 15: Here Are My Mother,
        Brothers, and Sisters .................... 91
Day 16: Zacchaeus ..................................... 95
Week 3 Conclusion .................................... 98

## week four

### Words about Our Relationship with God

Week 4 Memory Verse + Introduction ... 101
*Day 17:* The Greatest Commandment ... 103
*Day 18:* The Lord's Prayer ... 107
*Day 19:* Don't Worry ... 111
*Day 20:* Give to God What Is God's ... 115
*Day 21:* The Lost Son(s) ... 119
*Day 22:* The Pharisee and the Tax Collector ... 123
Week 4 Conclusion ... 126

## week five

### Words about Our Relationship with Others

Week 5 Memory Verse + Introduction .. 129
*Day 23:* Love Your Enemies ... 131
*Day 24:* Forgiving Others ... 135
*Day 25:* The Sheep and Goats ... 139
*Day 26:* The Good Samaritan ... 143
*Day 27:* Do Not Judge ... 147
*Day 28:* The Golden Rule ... 151
Week 5 Conclusion ... 154

## week six

### Jesus's Words on the Cost of Following Him

Week 6 Memory Verse + Introduction .. 157
*Day 29:* Jesus Must Suffer ... 159
*Day 30:* Deny Yourself, Take Up Your Cross, and Follow Me ... 163
*Day 31:* Serve Instead of Being Served .. 167
*Day 32:* This Is My Body and Blood ... 171
*Day 33:* Take This Cup Away from Me ... 175
*Day 34:* You Will See the Son of Man ... 179
Week 6 Conclusion ... 182

## week seven

### Jesus's Words from the Cross

Week 7 Memory Verse + Introduction .. 185
*Day 35:* Father, Forgive Them ... 187
*Day 36:* Today You Will Be with Me in Paradise ... 191
*Day 37:* Woman, Here Is Your Son ... 195
*Day 38:* Why Have You Abandoned Me? ... 199
*Day 39:* I'm Thirsty; It Is Finished ... 203
*Day 40:* Into Your Hands I Entrust My Spirit ... 207
Week 7 Conclusion ... 210
Conclusion— You Will Be My Witnesses ... 213

# Study Suggestions

*We believe that the Bible is true, trustworthy, and timeless and that it is vitally important for all believers. These study suggestions are intended to help you more effectively study Scripture as you seek to know and love God through His Word.*

## SUGGESTED STUDY TOOLS

- [ ] Bible

- [ ] Double-spaced, printed copy of the Scripture passages that this study covers (You can use a website like www.biblegateway.com to copy the text of a passage and print out a double-spaced copy to be able to mark on easily.)

- [ ] Journal to write notes or prayers

- [ ] Pens, colored pencils, and highlighters

- [ ] Dictionary to look up unfamiliar words

## HOW TO USE THIS STUDY

 ### Pray
Begin your study time in prayer. Ask God to reveal Himself to you, help you understand what you are reading, and transform you with His Word (Psalm 119:18).

 ### Read Scripture
Before you read what is written in each day of the study itself, read the assigned passages of Scripture for that day. Use your double-spaced copy to circle, underline, highlight, draw arrows, and mark in any way you would like to help you dig deeper as you work through a passage.

 ### Read Study Content
Read the daily written content provided for the current study day.

 ### Respond
Answer the questions that appear at the end of each study day.

# How to Study the Bible

*The inductive method provides tools for deeper and more intentional Bible study. To study the Bible inductively, work through the steps below after reading background information on the book.*

## Observation & Comprehension
**KEY QUESTION: WHAT DOES THE TEXT SAY?**

After reading the daily Scripture in its entirety at least once, begin working with smaller portions of the Scripture. Read a passage of Scripture repetitively, and then mark the following items in the text:

- Key or repeated words and ideas
- Key themes
- Transition words (e.g., therefore, but, because, if/then, likewise, etc.)
- Lists
- Comparisons and contrasts
- Commands
- Unfamiliar words (look these up in a dictionary)
- Questions you have about the text

## Interpretation
**KEY QUESTION: WHAT DOES THE TEXT MEAN?**

Once you have annotated the text, work through the following steps to help you interpret its meaning:

- Read the passage in other versions for a better understanding of the text.
- Read cross-references to help interpret Scripture with Scripture.
- Paraphrase or summarize the passage to check for understanding.
- Identify how the text reflects the metanarrative of Scripture, which is the story of creation, fall, redemption, and restoration.
- Read trustworthy commentaries if you need further insight into the meaning of the passage.

## Application
**KEY QUESTION: HOW SHOULD THE TRUTH OF THIS PASSAGE CHANGE ME?**

Bible study is not merely an intellectual pursuit. The truths about God, ourselves, and the gospel that we discover in Scripture should produce transformation in our hearts and lives. Answer the following questions and prompts as you consider what you have learned in your study:

- What attributes of God's character are revealed in the passage?
- Consider places where the text directly states the character of God, as well as how His character is revealed through His words and actions.
- What do I learn about myself in light of who God is?
- Consider how you fall short of God's character, how the text reveals your sin nature, and what it says about your new identity in Christ.
- How should this truth change me?
- A passage of Scripture may contain direct commands telling us what to do or warnings about sins to avoid in order to help us grow in holiness. Other times, our application flows out of seeing ourselves in light of God's character. As we pray and reflect on how God is calling us to change in light of His Word, we should be asking questions like, "How should I pray for God to change my heart?" and "What practical steps can I take toward cultivating habits of holiness?"

# The Attributes of God

### Eternal
God has no beginning and no end. He always was, always is, and always will be.
HAB. 1:12 / REV. 1:8 / ISA. 41:4

### Faithful
God is incapable of anything but fidelity. He is loyally devoted to His plan and purpose.
2 TIM. 2:13 / DEUT. 7:9 / HEB. 10:23

### Good
God is pure; there is no defilement in Him. He is unable to sin, and all He does is good.
GEN. 1:31 / PS. 34:8 / PS. 107:1

### Gracious
God is kind, giving us gifts and benefits we do not deserve.
2 KINGS 13:23 / PS. 145:8
ISA. 30:18

### Holy
God is undefiled and unable to be in the presence of defilement. He is sacred and set-apart.
REV. 4:8 / LEV. 19:2 / HAB. 1:13

### Incomprehensible
God is high above and beyond human understanding. He is unable to be fully known.
PS. 145:3 / ISA. 55:8-9
ROM. 11:33-36

### Immutable
God does not change. He is the same yesterday, today, and tomorrow.
1 SAM. 15:29 / ROM. 11:29
JAMES 1:17

### Infinite
God is limitless. He exhibits all of His attributes perfectly and boundlessly.
ROM. 11:33-36 / ISA. 40:28
PS. 147:5

### Jealous
God is desirous of receiving the praise and affection He rightly deserves.
EXOD. 20:5 / DEUT. 4:23-24
JOSH. 24:19

### Just
God governs in perfect justice. He acts in accordance with justice. In Him, there is no wrongdoing or dishonesty.
ISA. 61:8 / DEUT. 32:4 / PS. 146:7-9

### Loving
God is eternally, enduringly, steadfastly loving and affectionate. He does not forsake or betray His covenant love.
JOHN 3:16 / EPH. 2:4-5 / 1 JOHN 4:16

### Merciful
God is compassionate, withholding from us the wrath that we deserve.
TITUS 3:5 / PS. 25:10
LAM. 3:22-23

### Omnipotent

God is all-powerful;
His strength is unlimited.

MATT. 19:26 / JOB 42:1-2
JER. 32:27

### Omnipresent

God is everywhere;
His presence is near
and permeating.

PROV. 15:3 / PS. 139:7-10
JER. 23:23-24

### Omniscient

God is all-knowing;
there is nothing
unknown to Him.

PS. 147:4 / I JOHN 3:20
HEB. 4:13

### Patient

God is long-suffering and
enduring. He gives ample
opportunity for people
to turn toward Him.

ROM. 2:4 / 2 PET. 3:9 / PS. 86:15

### Self-Existent

God was not created
but exists by His
power alone.

PS. 90:1-2 / JOHN 1:4 / JOHN 5:26

### Self-Sufficient

God has no needs
and depends on
nothing, but everything
depends on God.

ISA. 40:28-31 / ACTS 17:24-25
PHIL. 4:19

### Sovereign

God governs over
all things; He is in
complete control.

COL. 1:17 / PS. 24:1-2
1 CHRON. 29:11-12

### Truthful

God is our measurement
of what is fact. By Him
we are able to discern
true and false.

JOHN 3:33 / ROM. 1:25 / JOHN 14:6

### Wise

God is infinitely
knowledgeable and
is judicious with
His knowledge.

ISA. 46:9-10 / ISA. 55:9 / PROV. 3:19

### Wrathful

God stands in opposition
to all that is evil. He enacts
judgment according to
His holiness, righteousness,
and justice.

PS. 69:24 / JOHN 3:36 / ROM. 1:18

# Timeline of Scripture

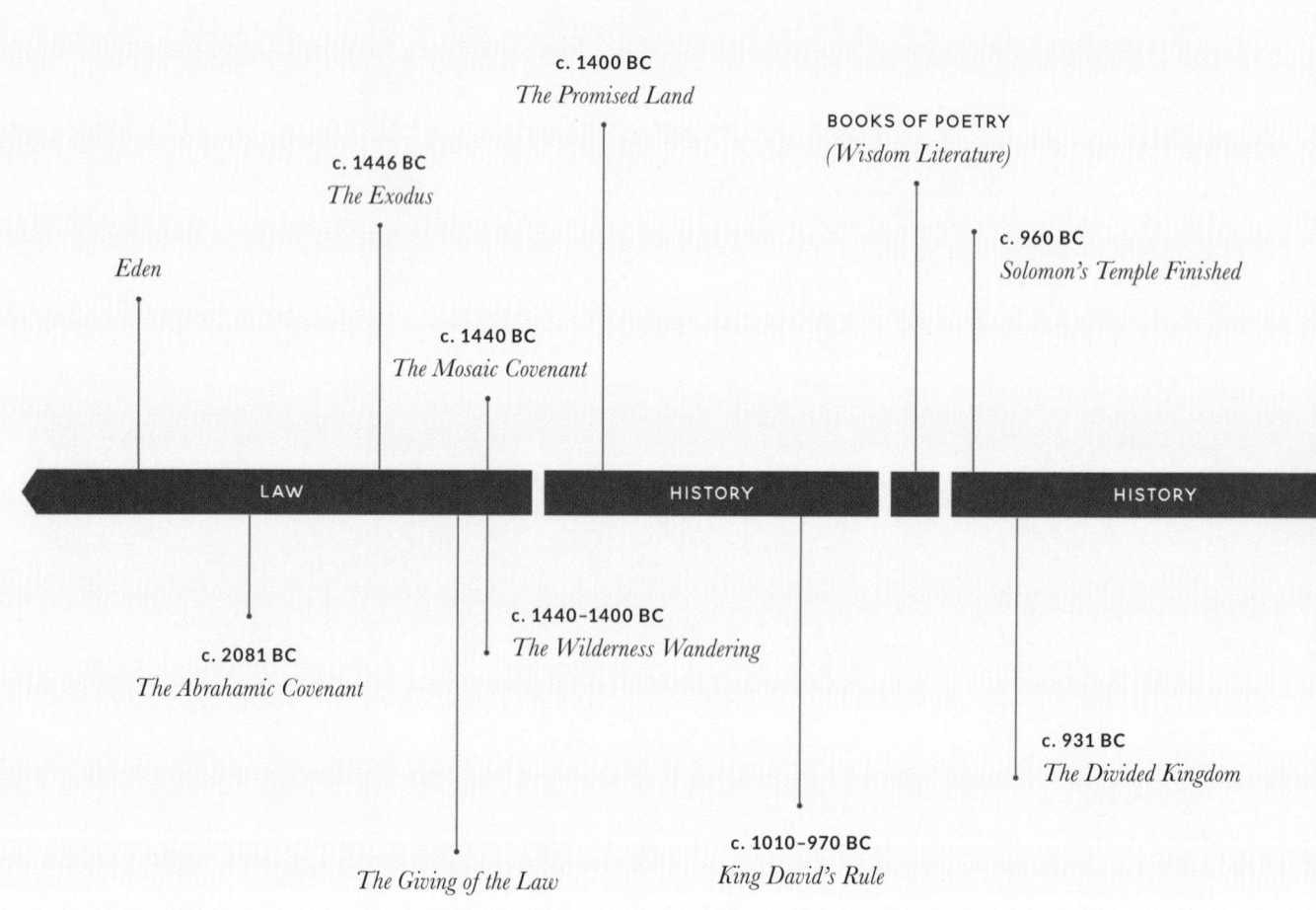

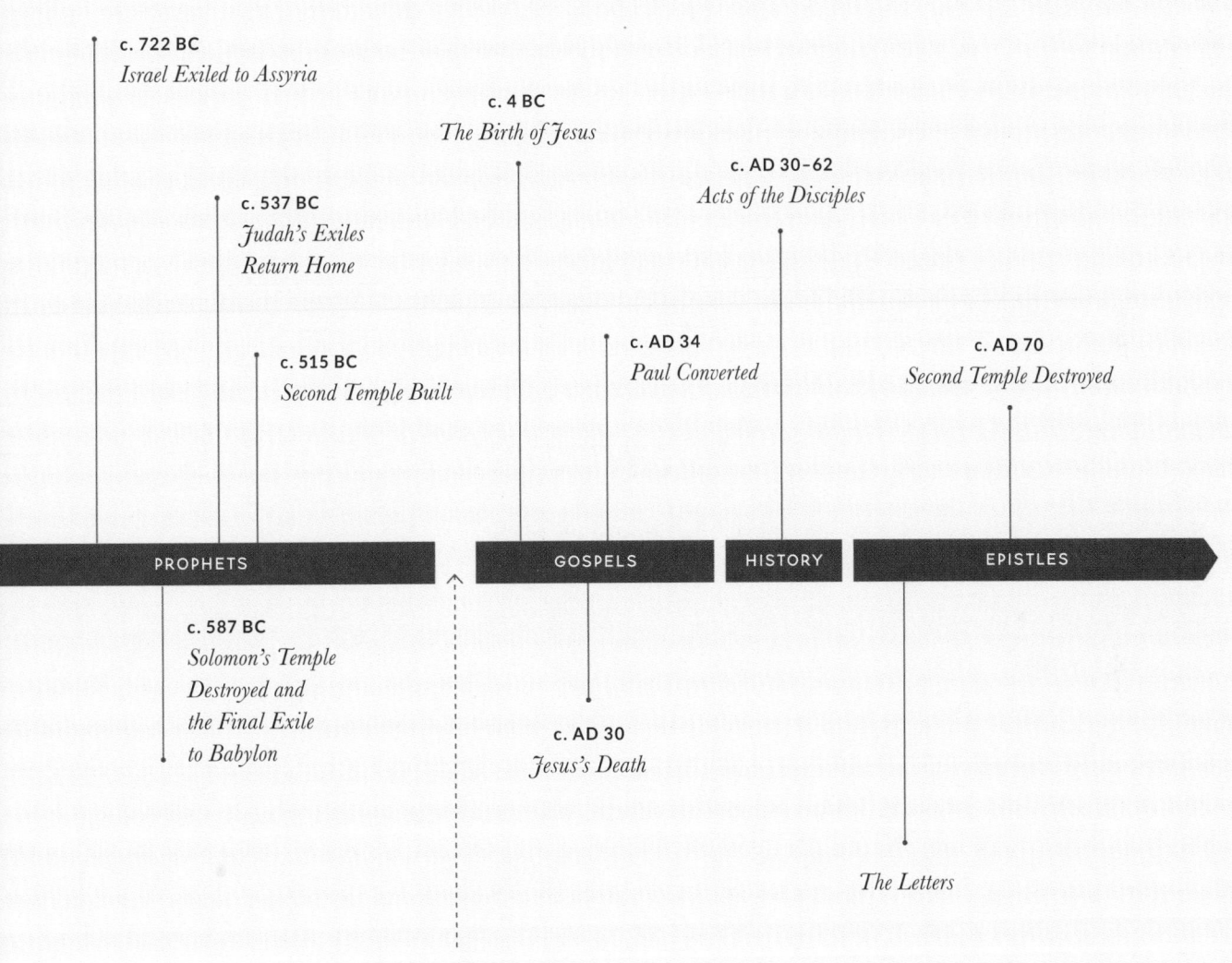

Timeline of Scripture / 13

# *Metanarrative* of Scripture

## Creation

In the beginning, God created the universe. He made the world and everything in it. He created humans in His own image to be His representatives on the earth.

## Fall

The first humans, Adam and Eve, disobeyed God by eating from the fruit of the Tree of Knowledge of Good and Evil. Their disobedience impacted the whole world. The punishment for sin is death, and because of Adam's original sin, all humans are sinful and condemned to death.

## Redemption

God sent His Son to become a human and redeem His people. Jesus Christ lived a sinless life but died on the cross to pay the penalty for sin. He resurrected from the dead and ascended into heaven. All who put their faith in Jesus are saved from death and freely receive the gift of eternal life.

## Restoration

One day, Jesus Christ will return again and restore all that sin destroyed. He will usher in a new heaven and new earth where all who trust in Him will live eternally with glorified bodies in the presence of God.

# How to Use This Study

Welcome to *'Tis So Sweet to Trust in Jesus: A 40-Day Journey to the Cross Through the Words of Christ*! Our prayer for you as you read through this study is that by reflecting on some of Jesus's most well-known words, you will grow in your love for Him and be encouraged as you seek to follow Him.

*'Tis So Sweet to Trust in Jesus* is a study designed to be used during Lent, the season that leads up to and prepares our hearts for Easter. That said, it is not essential to use this study during Lent. We hope this study will draw all who read it closer to Jesus, regardless of the time of year in which it is used!

### WHAT IS LENT?

For centuries, Christians all over the world have observed the season of Lent as a way to prepare their hearts for Easter. Lent is a season of self-examination, a kind of spiritual "spring cleaning." It is a season devoted to identifying the spiritual roadblocks in our lives (such as particular sins or practices that distract us from God), removing them, and replacing them with something beneficial. It is a time to "put off" the practices of the old self and "put on" the practices of the new (Colossians 3:9–10). In agreement with the old hymn, Lent acknowledges that we are "Prone to wander . . . prone to leave the God [we] love," and encourages us to recalibrate our spiritual lives.

To this end, many Christians practice some kind of fasting during Lent. The purpose of the fast is to create more space for God in our lives. Whether it is a fast from food or from a particular activity that tends to divert our attention away from the Lord, fasting is meant—in the words of Robert Webber—to "establish, maintain, repair, and transform our relationship with God" (Webber, 113). Webber goes on to describe fasting's effects as ridding ourselves of the toxins and poisons that inhibit spiritual growth.

Lent begins on Ash Wednesday and concludes on Holy Saturday, the day before Easter. This is technically forty-six days. But Christians have long refrained from fasting on Sundays since it is the day of Jesus's resurrection. Sunday is therefore a feast day, not a fast day. And so the forty days of Lent refer to the number of fasting days during this season. In summary, Lent involves turning from sin or other obstacles that distract us from Jesus and instead pursuing the practices that turn our hearts toward Jesus. Our prayer is that this journey through Jesus's words will help you do just that.

## ABOUT THIS STUDY

While *'Tis So Sweet to Trust in Jesus* does not need to be completed during Lent, it has been structured around the season of Lent. The first week will therefore be the shortest, beginning on Ash Wednesday and concluding on Saturday. In all, the study includes seven weeks, each containing sayings of Jesus that speak to a specific theme:

---

**WEEK 1 (DAYS 1–4)**
Words about What Jesus Came to Do

---

**WEEK 2 (DAYS 5–10)**
Jesus's "I Am" Statements

---

**WEEK 3 (DAYS 11–16)**
Words That Reveal Jesus's Heart

---

**WEEK 4 (DAYS 17–22)**
Words about Our Relationship with God

---

**WEEK 5 (DAYS 23–28)**
Words about Our Relationship with Others

---

**WEEK 6 (DAYS 29–34)**
Jesus's Words on the Cost of Following Him

---

**WEEK 7 (DAYS 35–40)**
Jesus's Words from the Cross

---

This is followed by a final, forty-first entry that can be read on Easter Sunday, which serves to wrap up the study and help you consider how to apply what you have learned moving forward.

Each entry will explore one of Jesus's sayings and unpack its significance for our understanding of Him. Also included are reflection questions, prayer prompts, and weekly introductions and summaries that help you appreciate the significance of these words for your own life.

We pray that this study will help you to treasure Jesus's words in your heart and grow in your love for Him!

Cut along the dashed line on the following page for a reversible art print and Lent schedule.

Cut along the dashed line on the previous page for a reversible art print and Lent schedule.

week 1

# Words about What Jesus Came to Do

## memory verse

The time is fulfilled, and the kingdom of God has come near. Repent and believe the good news!

**MARK 1:15**

## introduction

In the first four days of this study, we will look at four of Jesus's statements that speak to Jesus's mission in the world. The week is devoted to the question, "What did Jesus come to do?" While much could be said in response to this question, this week's sayings will serve as a summary response to that question. We will see that Jesus came to establish His kingdom, bring freedom, lay down His life for sinners, and gather followers. These themes will be further elaborated on in the following weeks.

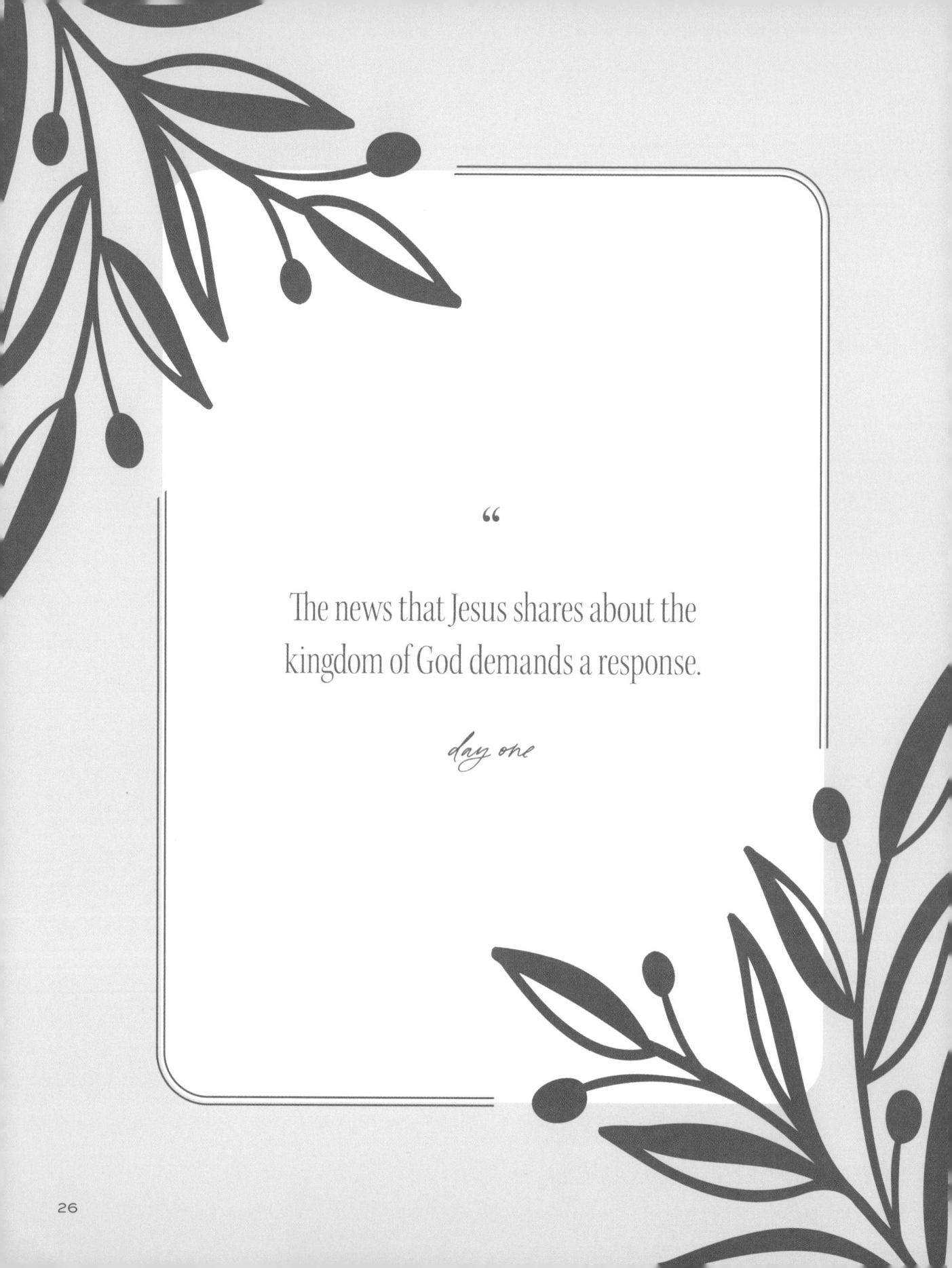

> "The news that Jesus shares about the kingdom of God demands a response.

*day one*

# Good News That Demands a Response

READ MARK 1:15

Life is full of news. Our smartphones give us constant news updates, from geopolitical conflicts halfway across the world to sales events from companies we follow. Much of the news we see on a daily basis is irrelevant to us and can be ignored.

But sometimes, we get news that demands a response. We learn that tickets for a highly anticipated concert are about to go on sale. We are told the date of a baby shower and invited to RSVP. Maybe a significant event happened near your city that you need to be aware of. In a similar way, the news that Jesus shares about the kingdom of God demands a response.

It is worth looking at some of the details Mark includes at the beginning of his Gospel. Mark starts with these words: "The beginning of the gospel of Jesus Christ, the Son of God" (Mark 1:1). The word "gospel" itself means "good news." And "Christ" (or "Messiah" in some translations) means "Anointed One," a reference to a future descendant of King David who would take His seat on David's throne and rule forever.

A few verses later, we read about Jesus's baptism. As Jesus is coming out of the water, God says, "You are my beloved Son," words taken from Psalm 2:7, which describe a King from David's line who would rule over not just Israel but all nations.

What Mark is showing us is that the promised King from David's line has arrived. The reason, then, that Jesus says that the "time is fulfilled, and the kingdom of God has come near" (Mark 1:15) is that He, the King, has come.

But is Jesus saying God's kingdom is present? Or that it is coming soon? Is it *here* or *near*? The answer is both! When Jesus ascended to heaven after His death and resurrection, He was enthroned as King (Acts 2:32–36). But as Christians, we wait with eager expectation for Him to return and wipe away every last trace of sin and its effects. So the kingdom is here, but we also wait for it to arrive in its fullness.

What should be our response to this news about the kingdom? Jesus tells us: "Repent and believe the good news!" (Mark 1:15). *Believe* that He is the King sent from God to rule over the world, and reorient our lives around this truth. *Repent* of—or turn away from—the ways we have rebelled against God, preferring to live our lives on our terms rather than His.

When a new ruler comes to power, it is always news. It could be *bad* news if the ruler is harsh and unjust. But as we will see throughout this study, Jesus is a kind, wise, and just ruler. And He is committed to our good. That *this* is the kind of King whose kingdom will one day fill the whole world is good news indeed. May we respond appropriately to this news each day of our lives.

"The kingdom is here, but we also wait for it to arrive in its fullness."

**REFLECT**

How can you live your life with a greater awareness of the fact that Jesus is King? How should this truth rearrange your priorities? What should it lead you to repent of?

**PRAY**

Give thanks to God for sending Jesus, the perfect King, and confess the ways you have sinned against God. Ask for God to help you live in obedience to King Jesus.

"

Jesus's arrival is good news for the outcasts. Through Him, those on the margins find acceptance with God and a place in His family.

*day two*

# Good News for the Poor

READ LUKE 4:18–19

Take a moment and think back on times in your life when you received some really good news. Maybe there was a time when you were worried about how you did on a test at school, only to get the news that you did great on it. Or maybe there was a time when you were anxious about how to pay some bill or expense, only to find out that you received a raise at work. Maybe you have awaited test results from a doctor with great fear, only to learn that you were fine.

How did it feel when you got that good news? To some extent, it probably felt liberating, like being released from something—fear, anxiety, etc.—that had bound you. With good news comes a sense of release, and as we will see today, release is exactly what Jesus brings to us.

After Jesus's baptism and His temptation in the wilderness, Luke records that He then returned "in the power of the Spirit" (Luke 4:14) to Galilee, where He taught in various synagogues. Jesus then comes to the synagogue of His hometown of Nazareth where, after being handed the scroll of Isaiah, He reads a passage, which describes a figure who has been anointed with the Spirit preaching "good news to the poor" (Luke 4:18). "Today," He says, "this Scripture has been fulfilled" (Luke 4:21).

In the Bible, "poor" can refer not just to one's economic status but also to the sense of helplessness and desperation that might come with it (see Psalm 14:6). This kind of desperation can be felt by all kinds of outcasts. Tax collectors, for example, were not financially poor, but they were hated by their fellow Jews and pushed to the margins (Luke 5:30–32). Such outcasts are often very aware of how much they need God and are thus receptive to Him.

And Jesus's arrival is good news for the outcasts. Through Him, those on the margins find acceptance with God and a place in His family. Though they may be helpless now, their fortunes will be reversed, and Jesus brings to them this good news. And as the Church, we are to continue the work of Jesus today. James, reflecting this point, writes that "Pure and undefiled religion before God the Father is this: to look after orphans and widows in their distress and to keep oneself unstained from the world" (James 1:27).

This passage reminds us that Jesus releases us from all that binds us. We experience that release now through the forgiveness of sin, the gift of the Holy Spirit, and through belonging to Christ's body, the Church. We help others to experience this as we tell them about Jesus and meet their needs. And we will experience this release in full when Jesus returns.

> "As the Church, we are to continue the work of Jesus today."

## REFLECT

How have you seen Jesus bring freedom to your life?
What troubles do you still long to be released from?

## PRAY

Pray that you would always be mindful of your neediness and of the freedom that Jesus has brought to you. Ask for opportunities to bring this good news to troubled people around you.

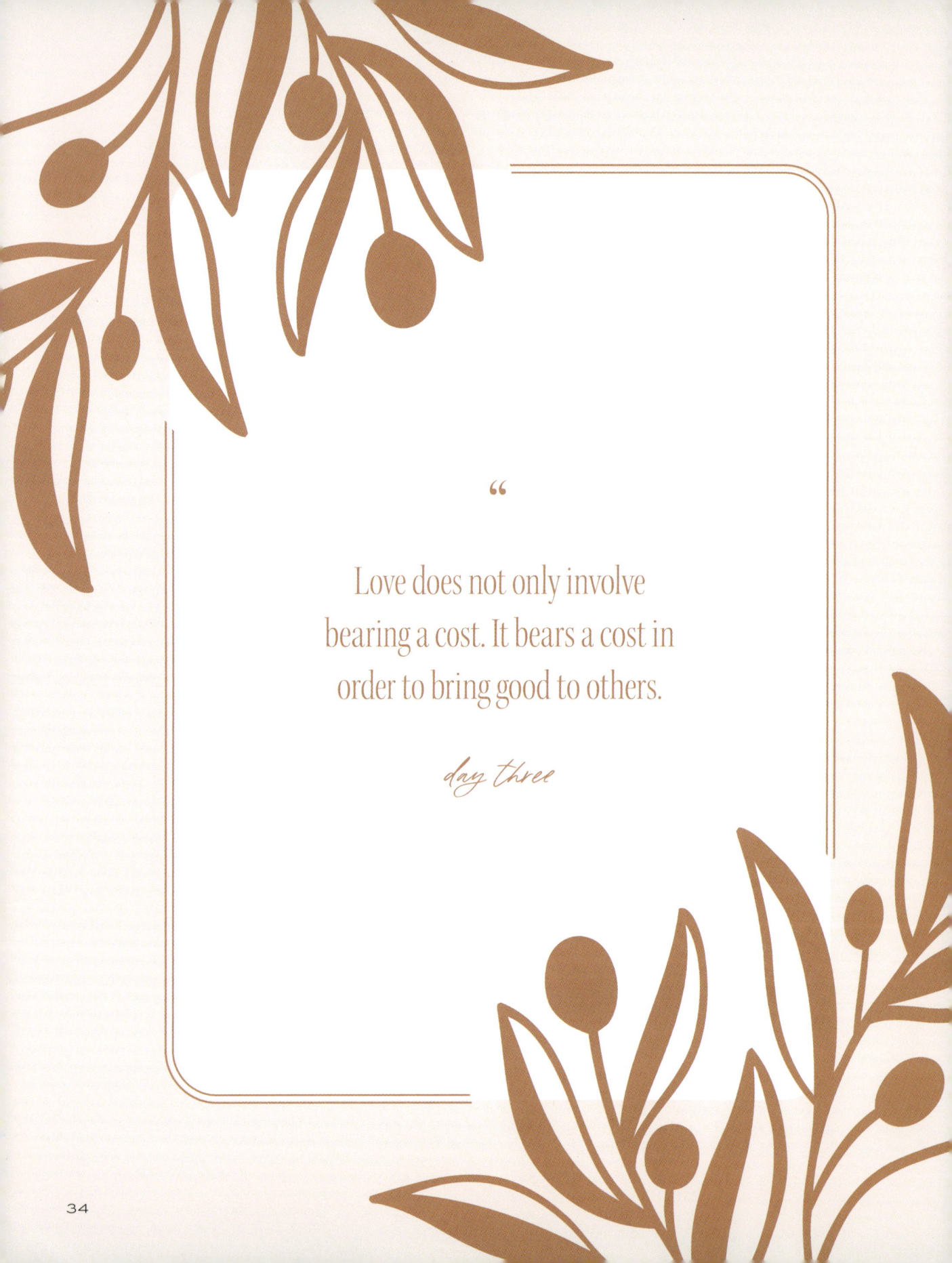

"
Love does not only involve bearing a cost. It bears a cost in order to bring good to others.

*day three*

# The Greatest Demonstration of God's Love

READ JOHN 3:16

Love. We all love it. We love to say and hear "I love you." Yet, actually demonstrating love can be tricky. If a person's *actions* do not communicate "I love you," it will mean very little when those words come out of their mouth.

What kinds of actions demonstrate love? Many answers could be given, but often, acts of love involve some level of cost. A parent reads to their child at night when they would rather collapse onto the couch. Someone spends their day off sitting with a friend who is hurting. You receive a thoughtful gift from someone who you know spent a long time intentionally picking the gift out and putting it together. Similarly, according to the Bible, the greatest demonstration of God's love for us is that He gave us His Son.

Out of His love for the world, God "gave his one and only Son." What does it mean that God "gave" His Son? Our minds may naturally think of this as referring to Jesus's death, and the verses right before this seem to confirm that (John 3:14–15). So, too, do other verses that describe how God demonstrates His love toward us through Jesus's death (Romans 5:8, 1 John 4:10).

But "gave" is not limited to Jesus's death. It also refers to His entire life. God "gave his one and only Son" in the sense that He sent Jesus into the world (John 3:17, 1 John 4:9). That the "Word [Jesus] became flesh and dwelt among us" is part of the costly love shown to us by God (John 1:14).

Philippians 2 captures this point well. After telling the Christians in Philippi to put the interests of others before their own, Paul then points to Jesus as a model of what he is urging them to do. He writes that although Jesus is equal with God, He humbled Himself by taking on a body, entering our world, and finally dying on the cross

(Philippians 2:5–11). Jesus inconvenienced Himself not only by dying on the cross but by experiencing firsthand what life in this world is like.

As Philippians 2 and John 3:16 point out, though, love does not only involve bearing a cost. It bears a cost in order to bring good to others. God gave His Son "so that everyone who believes in him will not perish but have eternal life." Simply put, Jesus is the greatest demonstration of God's love for us.

Commentator Bruce Milne captures the beauty of John 3:16 in these words: "If the depth of love is measured by the value of its gift, then God's love could not be greater, for his love-gift is his most precious possession—his only, eternally beloved Son. *He could not love more*" (77, emphasis added).

"Jesus is the greatest demonstration of God's love for us."

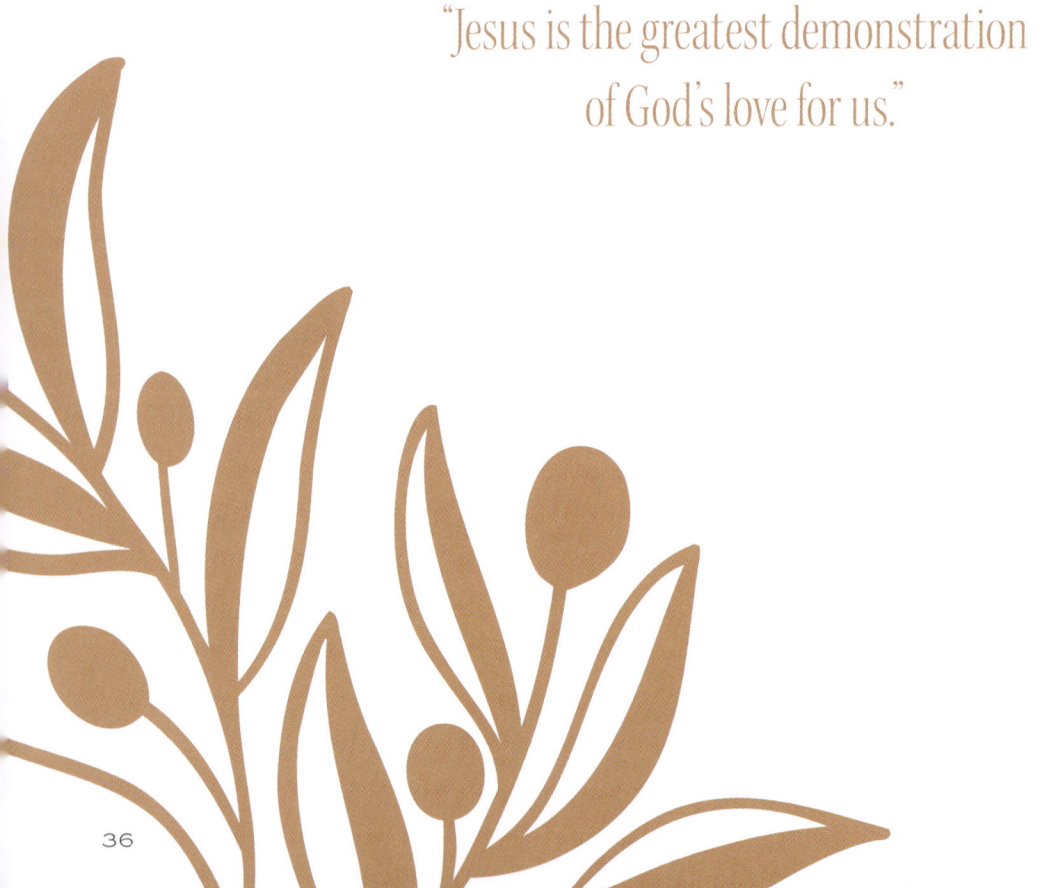

## REFLECT

When are you tempted to doubt that God loves you? Has the phrase "God loves you" ever felt more like a tired cliché than a truth to be savored? How can meditating on John 3:16 bring you comfort this week?

## PRAY

Ask for God to help you appreciate the magnitude of His love for you.

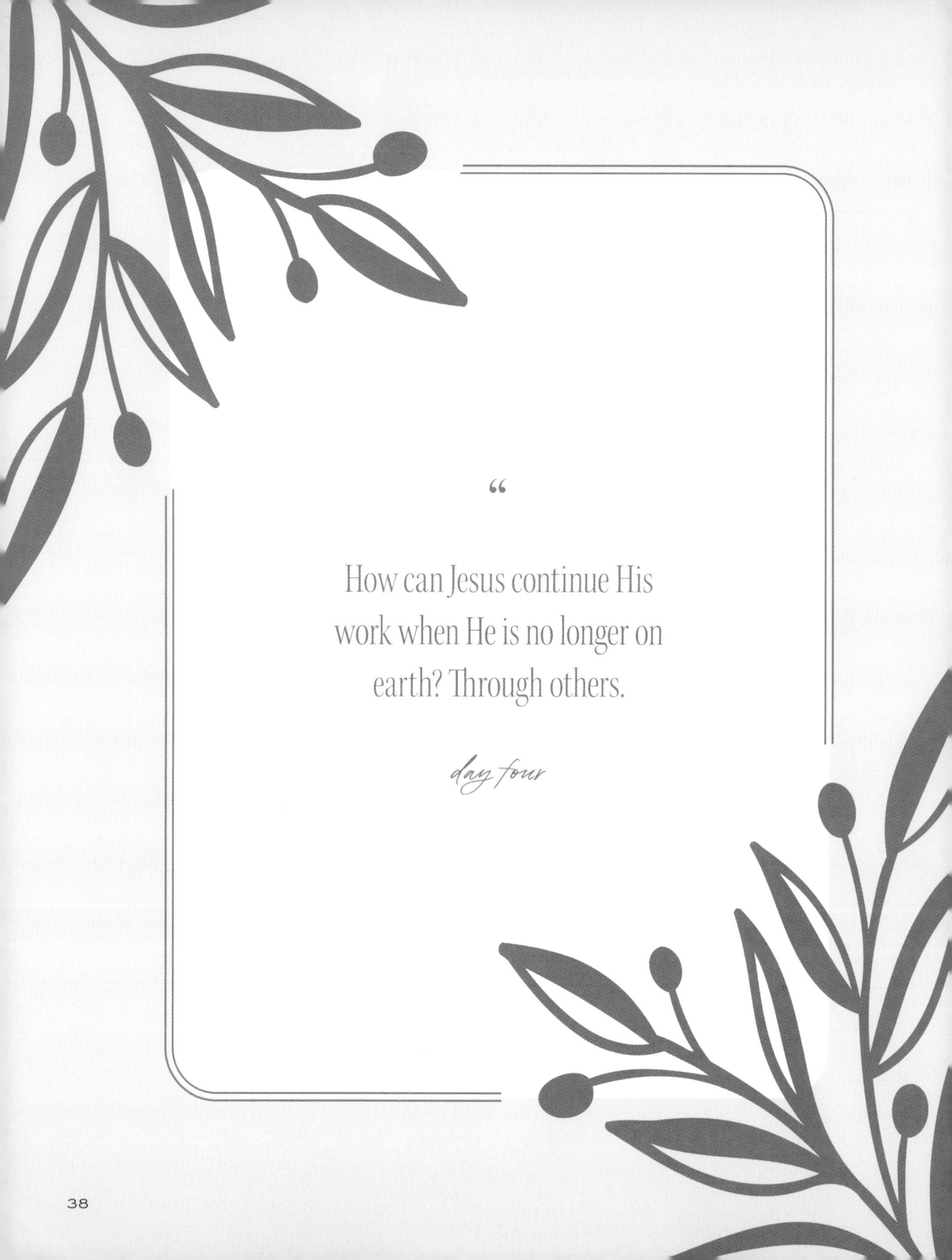

> How can Jesus continue His work when He is no longer on earth? Through others.

*day four*

# Follow Me

READ MARK 1:17

Before looking at Mark 1:17, it is worth looking briefly at the first verse of the book of Acts. In Acts 1:1, the author, Luke, mentions his "first narrative"—the Gospel of Luke—and describes it as a record of what "Jesus began to do and teach." The implication is that Acts is a record of what Jesus *continued* to do.

But how can Jesus continue His work when He is no longer on earth? Through others. Jesus's mission in the world is carried out not only by Himself but through His followers.

On Day 1 we looked at how Jesus went throughout Galilee proclaiming, "the kingdom of God has come near" (Mark 1:15). In the next scene of Mark's Gospel, we find Jesus walking along the Sea of Galilee, where He comes across a pair of brothers, Simon and Andrew, who are fishermen. After Jesus tells them to "Follow me," they drop their nets and do just that. Right after this, the same thing happens with another set of fishermen brothers, James and John, who respond to Jesus's summons by leaving their father and hired workers and following Him.

"Follow me." If someone were to come up and say these words to you today, how would you respond? You might assume they have something to show you or tell you, after which you could just go back to what you were doing. You might conclude that the interruption they are inviting you to is a brief one.

But Jesus is not calling these men to a brief interruption. Quite the opposite, in fact. By calling these men to "follow" Him, Jesus is telling them to become His disciples—to reorient their entire lives around Him and learn from Him. He is calling them to a life in which He takes precedence over all things that they may hold dear. It is an all-encompassing call.

What would make them do this?

In Mark 1, there is an emphasis on Jesus's authority. Further on, for example, the crowds are amazed at the authority with which He teaches them (Mark 1:22). They are similarly amazed at the authority with which He casts out demons (Mark 1:27). And here, when He tells Simon and Andrew to follow Him, it is not a request. The language is that of a command. He is issuing an order, which requires a response. Jesus speaks to these men with authority, and recognizing His authority, they respond to His words and devote their lives to Him.

Before ascending to heaven, Jesus commissioned His disciples to extend the call to "Follow me" far and wide, to make disciples of all nations (Matthew 28:18–20). To be a Christian today is to be a disciple — one who follows and learns from Jesus, one who values Him more than anything else in this world. And as we follow Him and show others how to do the same, we carry on Jesus's work in the world today.

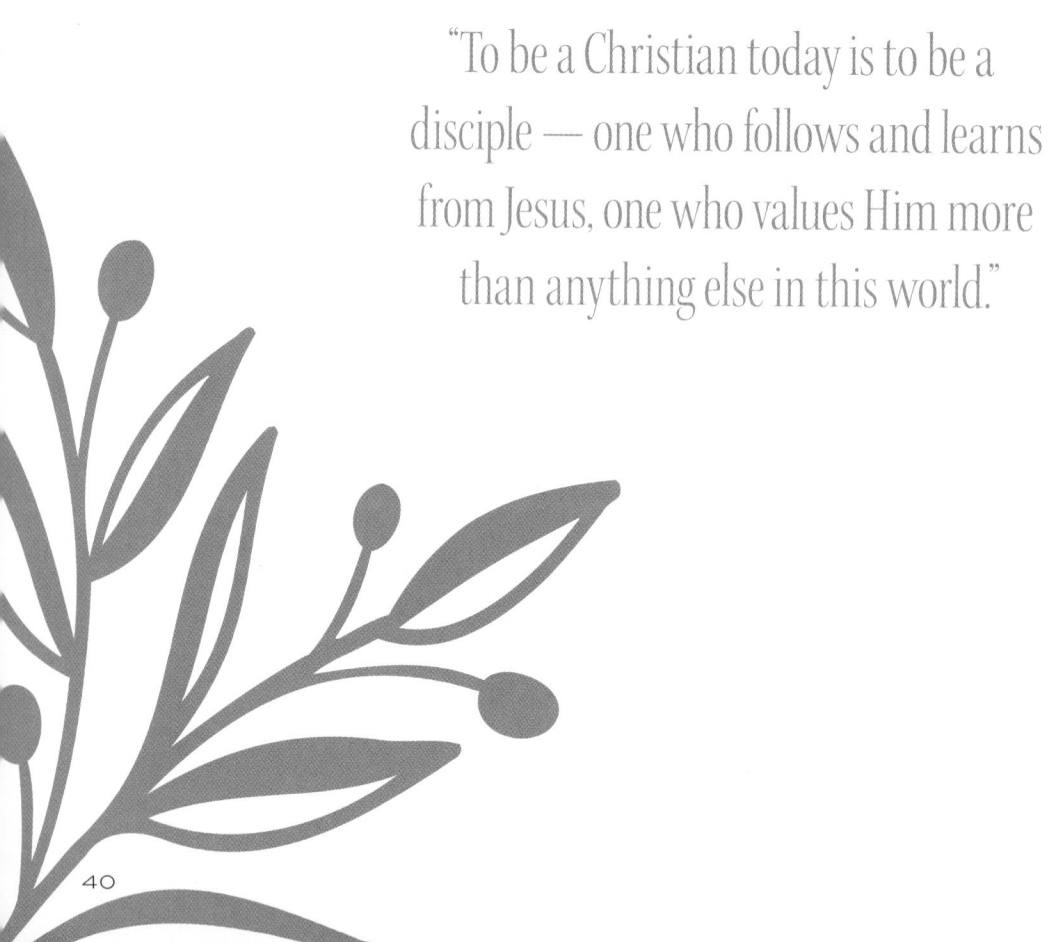

"To be a Christian today is to be a disciple — one who follows and learns from Jesus, one who values Him more than anything else in this world."

**REFLECT**

In your own words, how would you describe what it means to be a disciple of Jesus? How can you grow in your devotion to Him?

**PRAY**

Ask for God's help to be devoted to Jesus above all other things.

## week 1 conclusion

What did Jesus come to do? As a King, He came to begin His kingdom, a kingdom in which all that oppresses us in this life will be forever banished. He came to call followers who would take news of this King to the furthest ends of the earth. And citizenship in His kingdom is only possible because He also came to lay His life down in place of sinners. He gave up His life so that by faith in Him, we might live with Him forever. As you conclude this first week, take time to meditate on the fact that you have been "rescued . . . from the domain of darkness and transferred . . . into the kingdom" of Jesus (Colossians 1:13).

> As a King, He came to begin His kingdom, a kingdom in which all that oppresses us in this life will be forever banished.

*week 2*

# Jesus's "I Am" Statements

## memory verse

Jesus told him, "I am the way, the truth, and the life.
No one comes to the Father except through me."

**JOHN 14:6**

## introduction

In the book of Exodus, when God called Moses to bring the Israelites out of Egypt, and Moses asked God what His name was, God replied by saying, "I AM WHO I AM. This is what you are to say to the Israelites: I AM has sent me to you" (Exodus 3:14). Centuries later, in a move that shocked and enraged His opponents, Jesus claimed this name for Himself, saying, "Truly I tell you, before Abraham was, I am" (John 8:58). The Gospel of John also contains seven other statements in which Jesus says, "I am . . ." followed by a metaphor. These statements, which we will look at this week, underscore Jesus's divine nature and teach us important truths about who He is.

"

Jesus alone can satisfy the
deepest longings of our hearts.

*day five*

# The Bread of Life

READ JOHN 6:35

"If only _____."

Take a moment and consider how you might fill in that blank. What is something you want deeply?

Our lives are filled with desires that could be placed in that blank. On one end of the spectrum, we might think, *If only I could eat at my favorite restaurant tonight*, or *If only work were over so that I could go home and relax*. On the other end, our desires may be more weighty: *If only this relationship were healed* or *If only this grief would pass*. Reflecting on each "If only" we have is particularly appropriate as we consider the first "I Am" statement in John's Gospel. Through this statement, Jesus claims that only He can truly satisfy our deepest desires.

In John 6:1–15, Jesus miraculously feeds a crowd of thousands with just a few loaves of bread and two small fish. Afterward, the crowd—realizing that Jesus has crossed to the other side of the lake—follows after Him. But they are met with a gentle reprimand from Jesus, who tells them that they are only looking for Him because He has filled their stomachs. They have failed to consider what the miraculous feeding they have just experienced communicates about who He is. Their focus is on getting another free meal, but Jesus tells them to focus on "food that lasts for eternal life," another way of saying that they should believe in Him whom God has sent (John 6:26–29).

During this time, the Jewish people believed that when the Messiah arrived, He would provide bread (or "manna") from heaven, just as Moses had provided bread for Israel in the wilderness. After challenging Jesus to do this, Jesus responds by clarifying that *God* (not Moses) supplies bread from heaven and that He Himself is "the bread of life" (John 6:30–35).

Jesus's point is that physical food satisfies our stomachs—but only temporarily. Even lavish feasts that make us want to take a nap on the couch cannot keep us from becoming hungry again. But there is a deeper spiritual hunger in all of us that can be permanently satisfied when we come to—or believe in—Him. That we must "come" to Him means that apart from Him, this hunger will remain unsatisfied.

This is the hunger to know God, which as Jesus will say later, is eternal life (John 17:3). As the Son of God who pays for sins and establishes peace between us and God, Jesus alone can satisfy the deepest longings of our hearts. In Him is the emotional and spiritual wholeness we long for that we are often prone to look for in other places.

Beneath each "If only" we have is a deeper longing that only Jesus can satisfy. As the bread of life, Jesus nourishes our souls and satisfies us on the deepest level of our being.

> "As the bread of life, Jesus nourishes our souls and satisfies us on the deepest level of our being."

**REFLECT**

Jesus alone can truly satisfy the deepest longings of our hearts. How have you seen this to be true in your life? Why can't wealth, material comforts, pleasure, job promotions, accolades, etc., satisfy those desires? What "bread" besides Jesus are you tempted to hunger for?

**PRAY**

Ask for God to help you find your deepest satisfaction in Jesus.

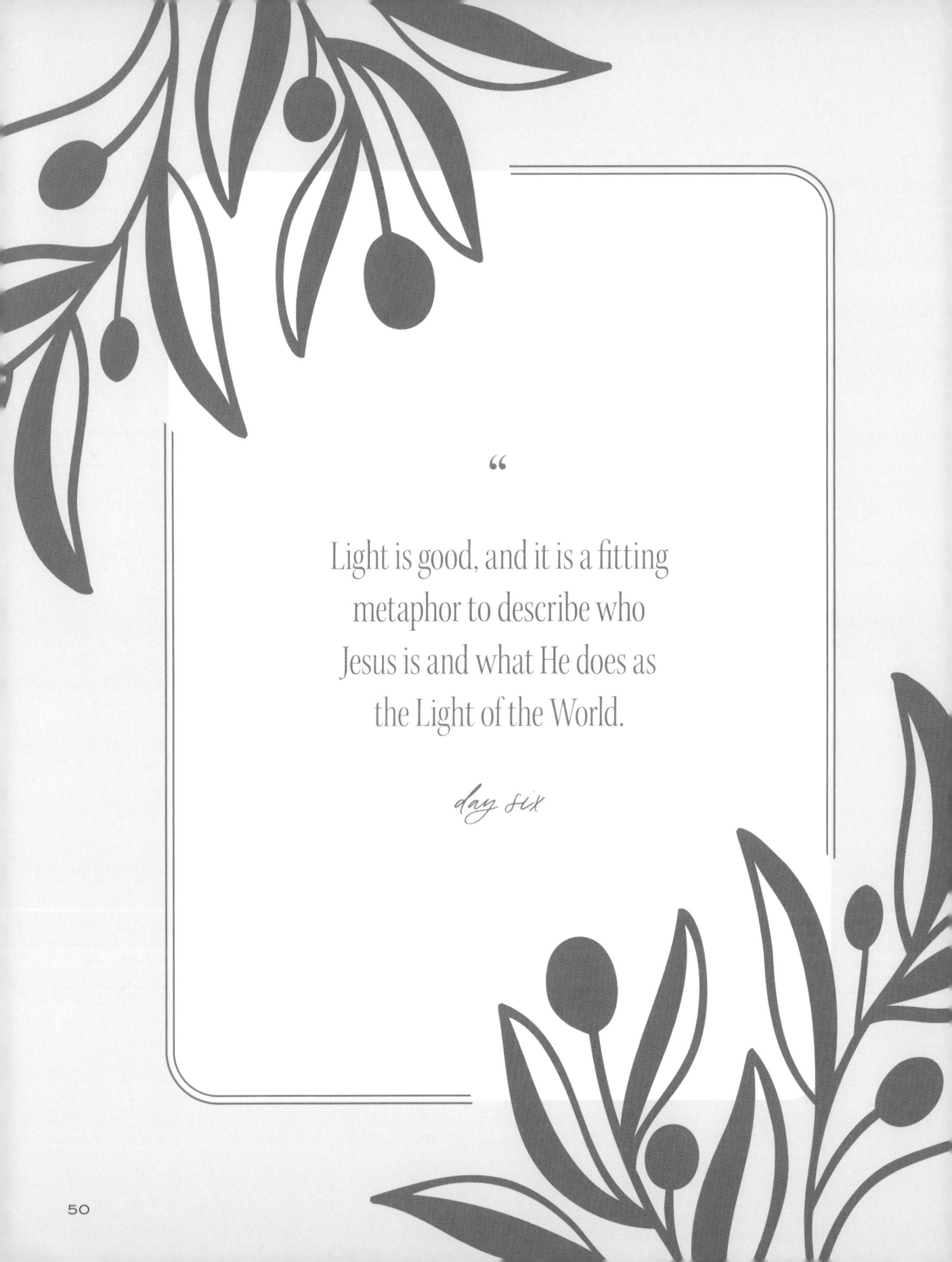

"

Light is good, and it is a fitting metaphor to describe who Jesus is and what He does as the Light of the World.

*day six*

# The Light of the World

READ JOHN 8:12

You have probably seen a character in a cartoon or comic strip think of a good idea. Their eyes grow wide. A smile forms. Maybe they snap their fingers. Then comes the universal sign of a good idea: a lightbulb appears above their head.

Light has long been used in metaphorical ways and usually positively—often to represent a good idea. We are "enlightened" when we learn something. When something has been clarified for us, our thoughts around that thing are "illuminated." People we enjoy "light up" our lives, and we talk about the "bright spot" of our day around the dinner table. Light is good, and it is a fitting metaphor to describe who Jesus is and what He does as the Light of the World.

In John 7, Jesus travels to Jerusalem for the annual Festival of Tabernacles, a seven-day celebration that commemorated Israel's wilderness wanderings and signaled the completion of the harvest. The seventh day of the festival included a water-pouring rite, possibly a reference to how God provided water from the rock for Israel in the wilderness. In this context, Jesus invites all who are thirsty to come to Him and receive "streams of living water" (John 7:37–39). What that water represents, in other words, is fulfilled in Him.

But the festival was also marked by a lighting ritual in which four large lamps would be lit, likely a reference to the pillar of fire that guided Israel in the wilderness and provided light for them at night. And just as He did with the water, Jesus points to Himself as the fulfillment of this rite, saying, "I am the light of the world" (John 8:12).

Light is associated with many things throughout the Bible. In addition to the pillar of fire guiding Israel (Exodus 13:21–22), the psalmist writes that the "Lord is my light and my salvation" (Psalm 27:1), and God's Word is described as "a lamp for my feet and a light on my path" (Psalm 119:105). Isaiah prophesies that God's servant would be "a light for the nations" and describes Israel's glorious future in terms of light (Isaiah 49:6, 60:19–22). By contrast, darkness in the Bible can represent walking away from God and destruction (Isaiah 59:9–10, Jeremiah 13:16).

We could, therefore, think of numerous ways that Jesus is "light." As the Word who has always existed and who took on flesh (John 1:1–2, 14), Jesus reveals to us what God is like. Through His teachings and His own example, He shows us how to live and how to experience God's salvation. And as the Light of the *World*, Jesus came to bring salvation to all nations and not just Israel.

As we follow the Light of the World, we "will have the light of life" and not walk in darkness (John 8:12). And as we reflect Jesus's light, we too will be lights in the world whose works will cause others to give glory to God (Matthew 5:14–16).

> "As we reflect Jesus's light, we too will be lights in the world whose works will cause others to give glory to God."

**REFLECT**

In what ways has Jesus brought light to your life?
How has He helped you to not walk in darkness?

**PRAY**

Thank God for revealing Himself to you through Jesus.
Ask for strength so that you may walk in His light
and reflect His light to others.

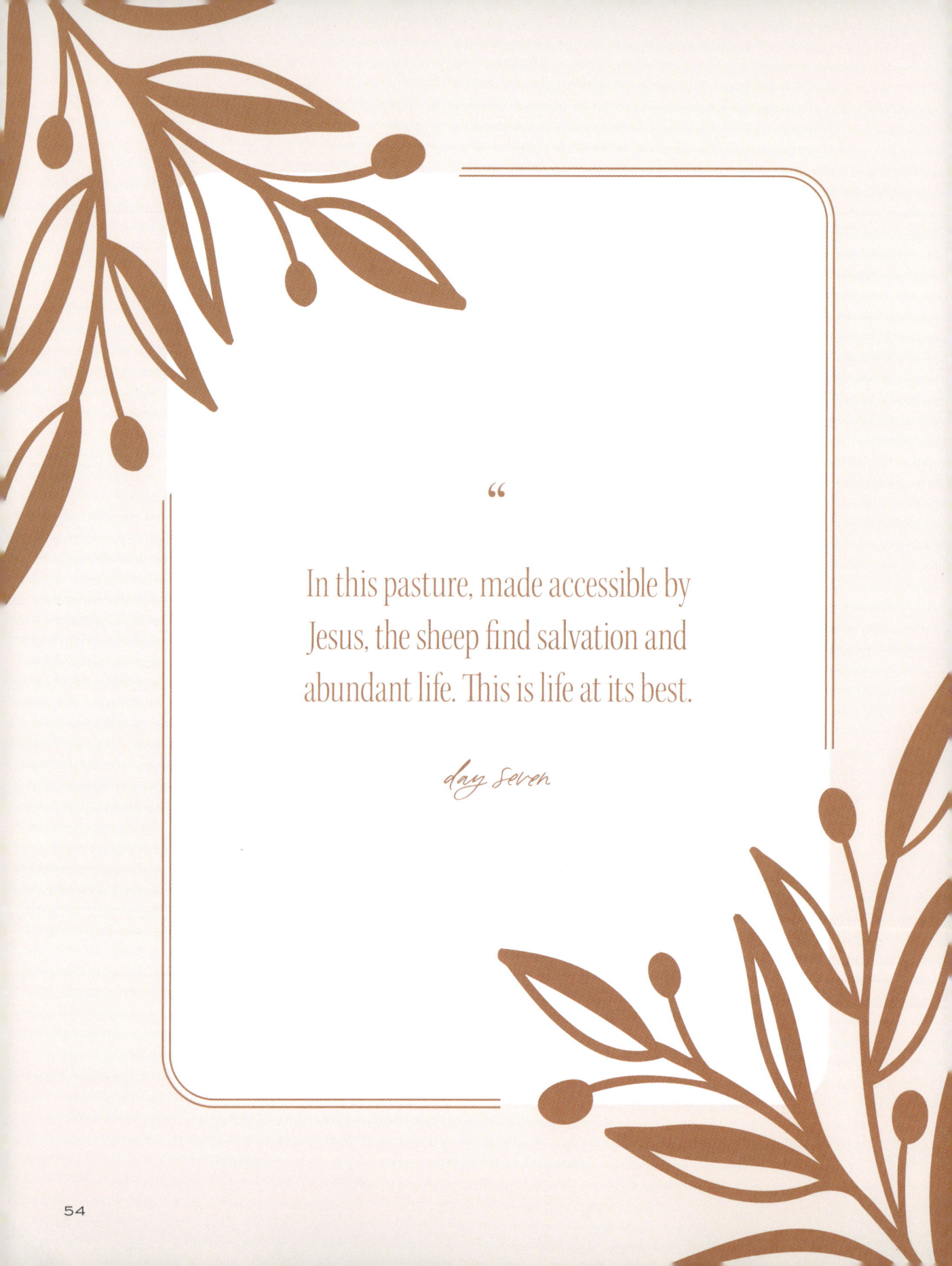

> In this pasture, made accessible by Jesus, the sheep find salvation and abundant life. This is life at its best.

*day seven*

# The Gate and the Good Shepherd

READ JOHN 10:7, 11

What comes to mind when you hear the phrase "the good life"? For some, that phrase might conjure images of sitting on a beach somewhere or being surrounded by scenic mountains. For others, it might simply look like a clean house or no responsibilities for a day. While these are all wonderful gifts of God to be enjoyed, Jesus shows us in John 10 that our lives are at their best when we experience His salvation and care. And He demonstrates this with metaphors taken from the world of shepherding.

The shepherd metaphor is a common one throughout Scripture, and it is often used in reference to God. David, for example, writes: "The Lord is my shepherd; I have what I need" (Psalm 23:1). God is the "Shepherd of Israel" who leads, protects, and carries them (Psalm 80:1, Isaiah 40:11).

The metaphor is also used negatively, however, to refer to Israel's corrupt leaders (Isaiah 56:9–12, Jeremiah 23:1–4, Zechariah 11:1–17). It is used this way extensively in Ezekiel 34, when God denounces the "shepherds" of Israel who have not cared for the people of Israel and have instead exploited them. In addition to judging these false shepherds who care only for themselves, God promises to come and shepherd the sheep Himself (Ezekiel 34:11–16).

The positive and negative uses of this metaphor come together in John 10. In the previous chapter, Jesus gave sight to a man who had been born blind, and the Pharisees, rather than celebrating with this man, interrogated him, insulted him, and threw him out of the temple. In response, Jesus utilizes this biblical metaphor and gives His next two "I Am" statements.

First, Jesus says, "I am the gate for the sheep" (John 10:7). In contrast to the Pharisees, who are "thieves" using the sheep for their own selfish ends, Jesus is the Gate through whom the sheep will flourish. In this pasture, made accessible by Jesus, the sheep find salvation and abundant life. This is life at its best.

But this kind of life is only possible because of what is communicated through the next "I Am" statement: "I am the good shepherd" (John 10:11). In contrast to the false shepherds of Ezekiel 34 and the Pharisees, Jesus perfectly embodies the care that a shepherd should have for his sheep — so much so that He willingly gives His life for them (John 10:15). Rather than using people for His own benefit, Jesus lays His life down to benefit others.

Can we imagine a better "good life" than this — a life in which we flourish under the care of a Shepherd who gave Himself for us; a Shepherd who knows us intimately and calls us by name (John 10:3, 14–15)? It is through Jesus alone, as the Good Shepherd and the Gate, that we can experience such attentive care both in this life and for eternity.

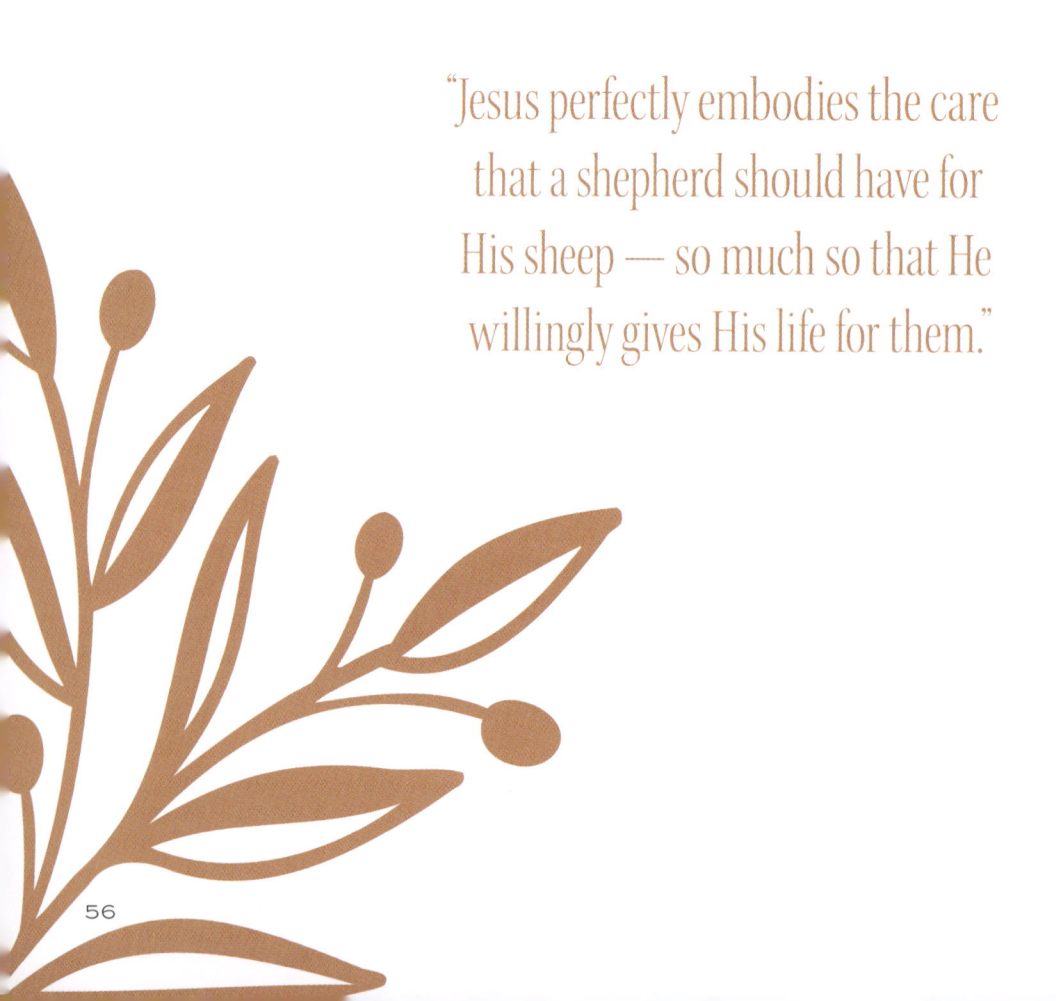

> "Jesus perfectly embodies the care that a shepherd should have for His sheep — so much so that He willingly gives His life for them."

**REFLECT**

Take a few minutes to reflect on these verses from John 10, as well as Psalm 23. What comfort and encouragement can you take from these passages today? When do you most need to be reminded that God is an attentive Shepherd?

**PRAY**

Ask for God to constantly remind you of His focused care for you, especially when times are hard.

> "Throughout John's Gospel, Jesus has spoken of His own role in this resurrection.

*day eight*

# The Resurrection and the Life

READ JOHN 11:25

In the 1987 film *The Princess Bride*, two beloved characters, Fezzik and Inigo, seek out a medicine man named Miracle Max. Their friend Westley has died, and they are hoping Max can perform a miracle. Max informs them that they are in luck because Westley is only "mostly dead." If Westley had been "all dead," the only thing left to do would be to "go through his pockets and look for loose change." To Max and many of us today, death is hopeless. But as we see in John 11, even the seemingly hopeless scenario of death is not permanent when Jesus is involved.

This is exactly the reminder that Mary and Martha need in John 11. These sisters, along with their brother Lazarus, were close to Jesus, so when Lazarus falls ill, they summon Jesus to come. Strangely, Jesus does not leave right away. In fact, it is *because* of His love for this family that Jesus waits (John 11:5–6). This delay will ultimately bring glory to God and the Son of God (verse 4), as well as bring belief for the disciples and others (verses 14–15, 45). And finally, His delay will benefit this family He loves.

When Jesus finally does arrive, He is approached by a grief-stricken Martha and assures her that Lazarus will rise again. This is not news to Martha. The Jews already believed that there would be a resurrection at the end of time, and Martha reflects this belief in her response (John 11:24).

But throughout John's Gospel, Jesus has spoken of His own role in this resurrection. *He* will raise up the dead on the last day (John 6:40); *He* gives life (John 5:21); *He*, like the Father, has life in Himself (John 5:26). Jesus reiterates these truths to Martha with His fifth "I Am" statement: "I am the resurrection and the life. The one who believes in me, even if he dies, will live" (John 11:25). Jesus wants Martha to focus not on this event at the end of history but on the One standing in front of her, the very One who will bring about that event.

To demonstrate the truth of what He is claiming about Himself, Jesus proceeds to raise Lazarus from death to life a few verses later. And this is where the significance of Jesus's delay is seen. There was a belief during this time that a dead person's soul would stay near their body for three days, hoping to enter into it again. By waiting until the fourth day to perform this miracle, Jesus shows that Lazarus is not just "mostly dead." He has started to decompose. Yet at the voice of Jesus—the resurrection and the life—Lazarus walks out of his own tomb.

And that is our future as well. Death may be inevitable, but it is not permanent. The day that Jesus and Martha spoke of is coming, and on that day, we, too, will respond to Jesus's voice and rise from our tombs to live with Him forever.

> "Death may be inevitable, but it is not permanent."

**REFLECT**

What comfort does this "I Am" statement give to you?
How can you comfort others with what Jesus says in John 11?

**PRAY**

Give thanks to God that because of Jesus, death is not the end.
Pray that you might live your life always mindful of your future resurrection.

"
Jesus alone can bring sinners
into the presence of God.

*day nine*

# The Way, the Truth, and the Life

READ JOHN 14:6

Have you ever felt like you lacked the necessary information to do something? You are asked to perform some task yet have no idea how to do it. You are invited to a party but not told when or where it will be. You are told the rules of a board game, only for those rules to go over your head. This is how one of Jesus's disciples, Thomas, felt in a conversation just before Jesus's death. And in His response to Thomas's confusion, Jesus makes the important point that He alone can bring people to God.

In John 14, Jesus is speaking to His disciples and preparing them for His departure. Though they are naturally troubled at the thought of His absence, Jesus wants to assure them that His departure will benefit them because He is leaving to prepare a place for them (John 14:2–3). He also assures them that He will come back for them and that they know the way to the place He is going (verses 3–4). To this, Thomas responds, *Actually, we don't*. His point is fair. How can one possibly know the way to a destination when they don't even know what the destination is?

In response, Jesus gives His sixth "I Am" statement: "I am the way, the truth, and the life. No one comes to the Father except through me" (John 14:6). Jesus is departing to prepare a place for His disciples in the presence of His Father. And Jesus does not merely *know* the way to that place, but He Himself *is* the way there. Jesus alone can bring sinners into the presence of God. Peter communicates this same point in the book of Acts when he says, "There is salvation in no one else, for there is no other name under heaven given to people by which we must be saved" (Acts 4:12).

Of the three things Jesus says about Himself in John 14:6, it seems that—given the context—"the way" is His primary claim, while "the truth" and "the life" support that claim. In other words, why is Jesus the only Way to God? Because He is the Truth and the Life. As the Truth, Jesus makes the Father known (John 1:18, 14:9, Hebrews 1:3). As the Life, Jesus—possessing life in Himself (John 5:26)—bestows eternal life to those who believe in Him (John 3:16, 11:25).

As God's creatures, we were made to live in His presence, yet as sinners, we are unable to approach Him on our own. But God does not leave us without a doorway to Him—we do not have to remain in a state of confusion, wondering where we should go or whom we should turn to. Through Christ, the way to God's presence has been opened. He alone brings us into the presence of God. It is through Jesus that God is made known, that sins are forgiven, and eternal life is received.

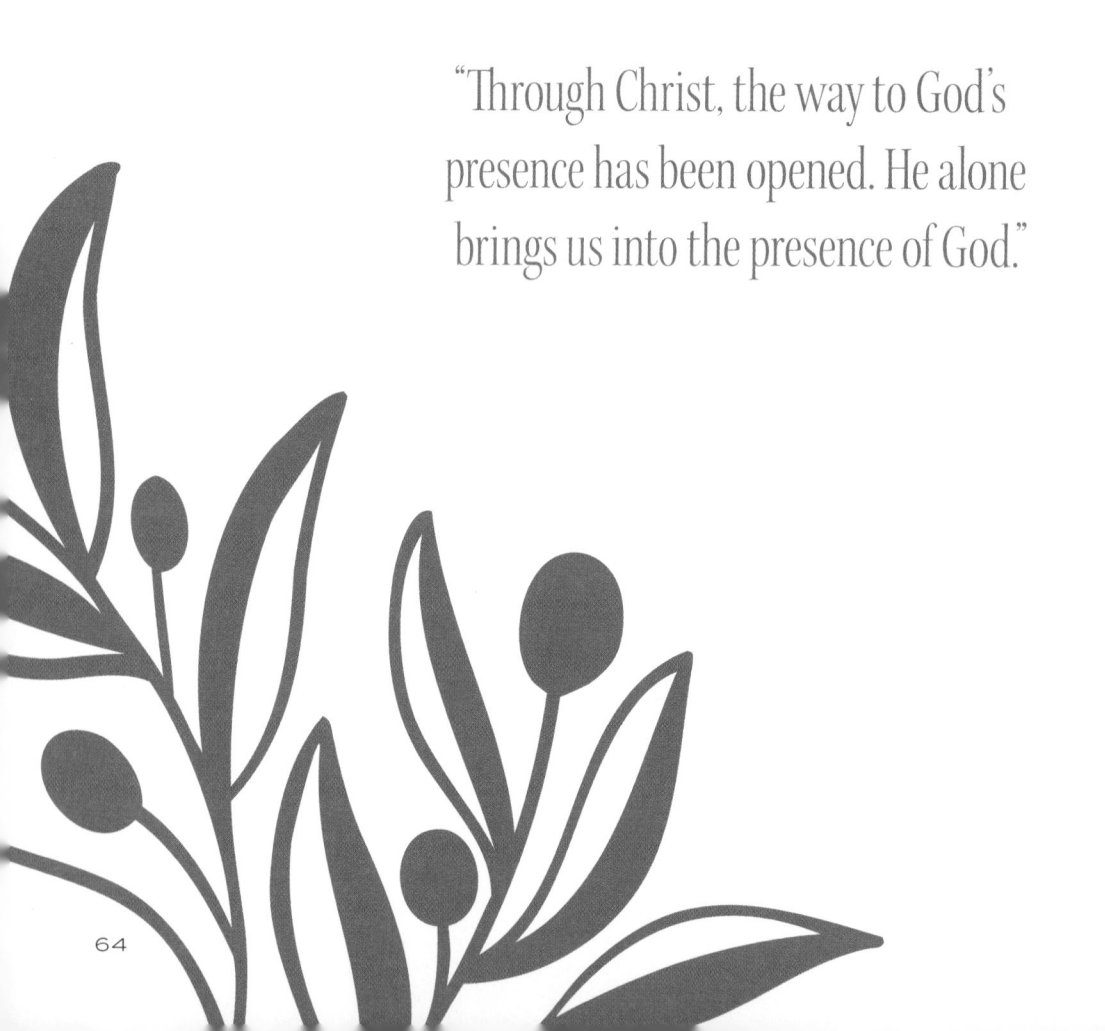

> "Through Christ, the way to God's presence has been opened. He alone brings us into the presence of God."

**REFLECT**

How can this "I Am" statement encourage us when we feel unworthy to approach God in prayer?

**PRAY**

Give God thanks for getting involved in our world and revealing Himself to us through Jesus.

> The vine metaphor illustrates the intimate, organic relationship that exists between Jesus and His followers.

*day ten*

# The True Vine

READ JOHN 15:1

The seventeenth-century *Westminster Shorter Catechism* begins by asking, "What is the chief end of man?" It answers by saying that our chief end (or purpose) is "to glorify God, and to enjoy him forever." We can glorify God in many ways (e.g., praying, singing, sharing our faith), but one central way is to reflect Him—to make Him known to the world around us. And as Jesus demonstrates in John 15, reflecting God to the world is what will happen as we are united to Him.

In John 15, Jesus continues to prepare His disciples for His departure. During this conversation—which spans chapters 13 through 16—Jesus has been comforting His disciples, telling them not to be afraid or troubled by His imminent departure. And now He begins to focus on the mission He is calling His disciples to after He leaves. In this context, Jesus gives the seventh and final "I Am" statement in John's Gospel: "I am the true vine . . ." (John 15:1).

"Vine" here is a loaded metaphor. In the Old Testament, the nation of Israel is frequently compared to a vine (Isaiah 5:1–7, Psalm 80:8–11, Jeremiah 2:21). But this comparison is often negative: Israel was a vine that was supposed to bear fruit but did not. Though God had called them to reflect Him to the nations, Israel instead ended up worshiping the false gods of those nations. But as the "true vine," Jesus will succeed where the nation of Israel had failed. Though they did not produce fruit, He will.

Just as God had planted and cultivated the vine in Isaiah 5:1–7, so here He cultivates the true Vine to ensure that its branches bear fruit (John 15:1–2). And who are the branches? Jesus's disciples (John 15:4–5). The vine metaphor illustrates the intimate, organic relationship that exists between Jesus and His followers. As we remain in

Jesus—by obeying His commands and loving Him and others (John 15:4, 9–10)—we will "produce much fruit and prove to be [His] disciples" (John 15:8).

And "by this," Jesus says, will His "Father [be] glorified" (John 15:8). At several points in this section of John, Scripture tells us that the Father is glorified in Jesus (13:31, 14:13, 17:4). So here, we see that one way Jesus brings glory to the Father is through us. As we depend on Jesus, learn from Him, live in obedience to His commands, demonstrate His care for others, and make Him known to the nations (see Matthew 28:18–20), we are fulfilling our "chief end" of glorifying and enjoying God.

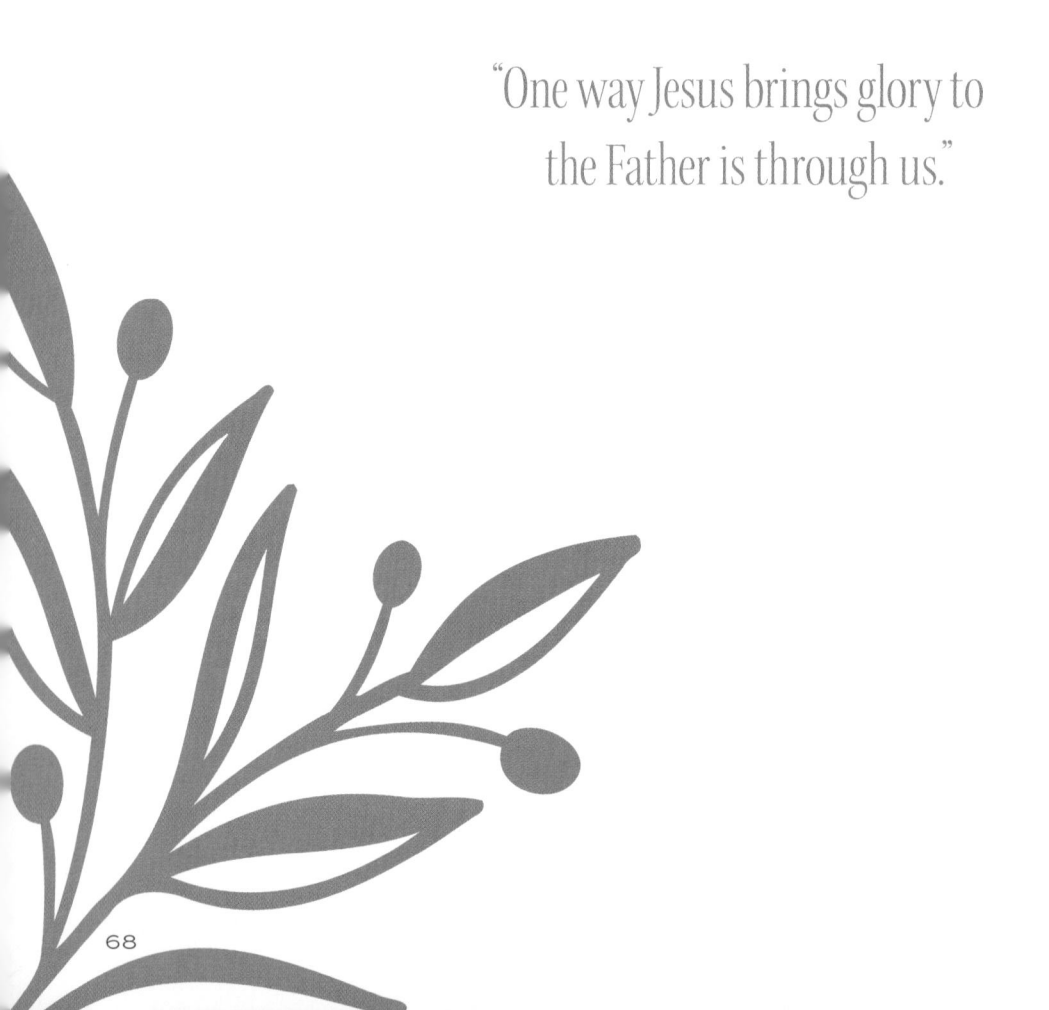

> "One way Jesus brings glory to the Father is through us."

**REFLECT**

In your own words, how would you describe the relationship between a vine and its branches? How does this metaphor help you to appreciate your relationship with Jesus?

**PRAY**

Pray that you would draw close to Jesus and bear fruit for the good of others and the glory of God.

*week 2 conclusion*

Who is Jesus? He is the Bread of Life, who satisfies our deepest desires. He is the Light of the World, who leads us out of the darkness. He is the Gate and the Good Shepherd, who protects and cares for us. He is the Resurrection and the Life, the One who shows us that death is not the end and who will raise us up from death to everlasting life. He is the Way to God. And He is the true Vine, who bears fruit in the world through us and brings glory to God. As you end this week, take time to sit and adore Jesus by reflecting on these truths.

> Who is Jesus? He is the Bread of Life,
> who satisfies our deepest desires.

*week 3*

# Words That Reveal Jesus's Heart

## memory verse

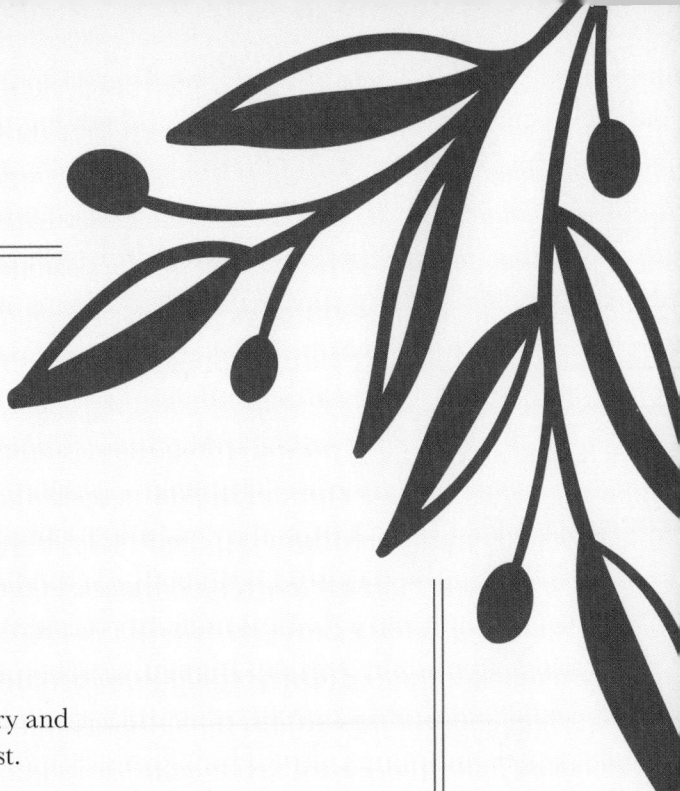

Come to me, all of you who are weary and
burdened, and I will give you rest.

MATTHEW 11:28

## introduction

What is Jesus like? That can be a challenging question to answer succinctly, and it is the question we will be considering this week. The statements we will be looking at demonstrate what Jesus is like by looking at what is important to Him. More specifically, we will see Jesus's perspective on groups of people who were often not highly valued in His day, reflect on what it means to be part of God's family, and dwell on what Jesus offers to those who come to Him. Prepare for this week by reflecting on times when you may have felt like an outcast or times when you have felt unworthy of God's love.

"

God's kingdom is different from
the kingdom of this world,
for it is the humble and lowly
who are truly blessed.

*day eleven*

# The Beatitudes

READ MATTHEW 5:3-10

Our world often tends to favor the powerful and the elite. Those "on top" receive the most praise and attention. We can experience this reality in our own lives. The popular employee gets the raise instead of us, even though it seems we have performed better. Our parents might favor our sibling more because of the awards they win or the grades they earn. These experiences might make us wonder if God treats us the same way, whether God favors the one who is the most competent, rich, and successful. But in Matthew 5:3–10, we learn that God's kingdom is different from the kingdom of this world, for it is the humble and lowly who are truly blessed.

Matthew 5:3–10 opens up what is called the "Sermon on the Mount," and in this sermon, Jesus focuses on what it looks like to live for God's kingdom. In the opening of this sermon, Jesus declares a series of blessings, referred to as "beatitudes." The word "blessed" in these verses describes someone who is well-off and happy. Again, we might think that it is those who have an abundance of possessions or accolades who are blessed, but this is not what Jesus says. Jesus says that, among others, it is the poor in spirit, the mourners, the humble, the persecuted, and the merciful who are blessed. Not only this, but these types of people possess the kingdom, inherit the earth, and are called sons of God.

So who are these people exactly? They are disciples of Jesus. They are those who recognize their need for Jesus and depend on Him. They are those who mourn over the brokenness of this world and look to Jesus for hope. They are those who seek after righteousness rather than unrighteousness. Jesus is not saying in these passages that the wealthy or someone in a high position cannot follow Him. Rather, Jesus is teaching that any person who humbles their heart and seeks to live for God's kingdom will receive the greatest blessings—forgiveness, a relationship with God, and entrance into God's kingdom. All of these blessings are a gift of Christ's grace bestowed upon those who place their faith in Him.

Jesus's words in this passage reveal His heart. He is not like those in our world who favor the elite. He does not focus His attention only on those who are the most powerful. Jesus recognizes humble hearts, hears the cries of those who mourn, and gives hope to the persecuted. The Beatitudes remind us as believers that it is followers of Christ who are truly blessed. Whether we have much or little in this life, we are well off because we have received salvation and eternal life. We belong to God's kingdom and are called children of God. No worldly success compares to the true blessing that comes from being a follower of Christ.

> "Jesus recognizes humble hearts, hears the cries of those who mourn, and gives hope to the persecuted."

**REFLECT**

How have you seen Jesus's blessings in your life?

**PRAY**

Ask God to continually give you a humble heart and to keep seeking His kingdom over the kingdom of this world.

"

Rest is not found in having *no* burdens,
but in taking on the right burden.

*day twelve*

# I Will Give You Rest

READ MATTHEW 11:28-30

In *The Pilgrim's Progress*—John Bunyan's allegory of the Christian life—the main character, Christian, carries a burden on his back, representing his sin and guilt. Upon coming to the cross where Jesus died, "his burden came loose from his shoulders and fell off his back . . ." (Bunyan, 49). It is a powerful picture of the truth that in the presence of Jesus, our burdens are removed, and we find freedom.

People in Jesus's day knew about burdens. Later in Matthew, for example, Jesus warns people about the Pharisees and scribes who "tie up heavy loads that are hard to carry and put them on people's shoulders" (Matthew 23:4). Through their extensive supplemental laws meant to safeguard the people's observance of Old Testament commands, the Pharisees had made obedience to God a matter of endless rules. And on top of this burden was the steady stream of everyday burdens that come with living in a fallen world.

Jesus extends this offer of rest to these burdened people in Matthew 11:28. Surprisingly, though, Jesus then invites them to take His yoke upon them (Matthew 11:29). A "yoke" was a wooden frame placed on animals to carry burdens, and it was often used as a metaphor for one's commitment to observe the Old Testament law. Jesus is saying that people find rest when they come to Him and swap out one type of yoke for another. Rest is not found in having *no* burdens but in taking on the right burden.

But the yoke Jesus offers "is easy and [His] burden is light" (Matthew 11:30). Again, this might seem surprising, since Jesus elsewhere discusses how costly it is to be His disciple (Matthew 10:37–39) and how He has not come to relax the Law's demands in the slightest (Matthew 5:17–20). The difference, though, is that with Jesus's yoke comes the ability to bear it.

Commentator Robert Mounce writes, "Although the requirements of the kingdom are great, they appear in a different light when seen as expressions of loving obedience rather than demands for religious achievement. . . . The burden he asks us to bear is light in that it is not obedience to external commandments but loyalty to a person" (Mounce, 109). This person is Jesus.

Through Jesus, the burden of our sins has been removed. And with that, so too has the burden of trying to please God in our own effort out of a sense of duty. In its place, we have received the burden of God's approval and the Holy Spirit who helps us to obey God's commands out of love. And though we still deal with various burdens or hardships in our day-to-day lives, we also carry the burden of knowing that Jesus is with us through them all (Matthew 28:20).

> "Through Jesus, the burden of our sins has been removed."

**REFLECT**

In what ways do you feel burdened right now? How can Jesus's words in Matthew 11:28–30 comfort you when you encounter life's many trials?

**PRAY**

Ask that God would help you enjoy the rest that He provides for you, and pray that Jesus will come again soon, that you might experience the rest that will be found in a whole new earth.

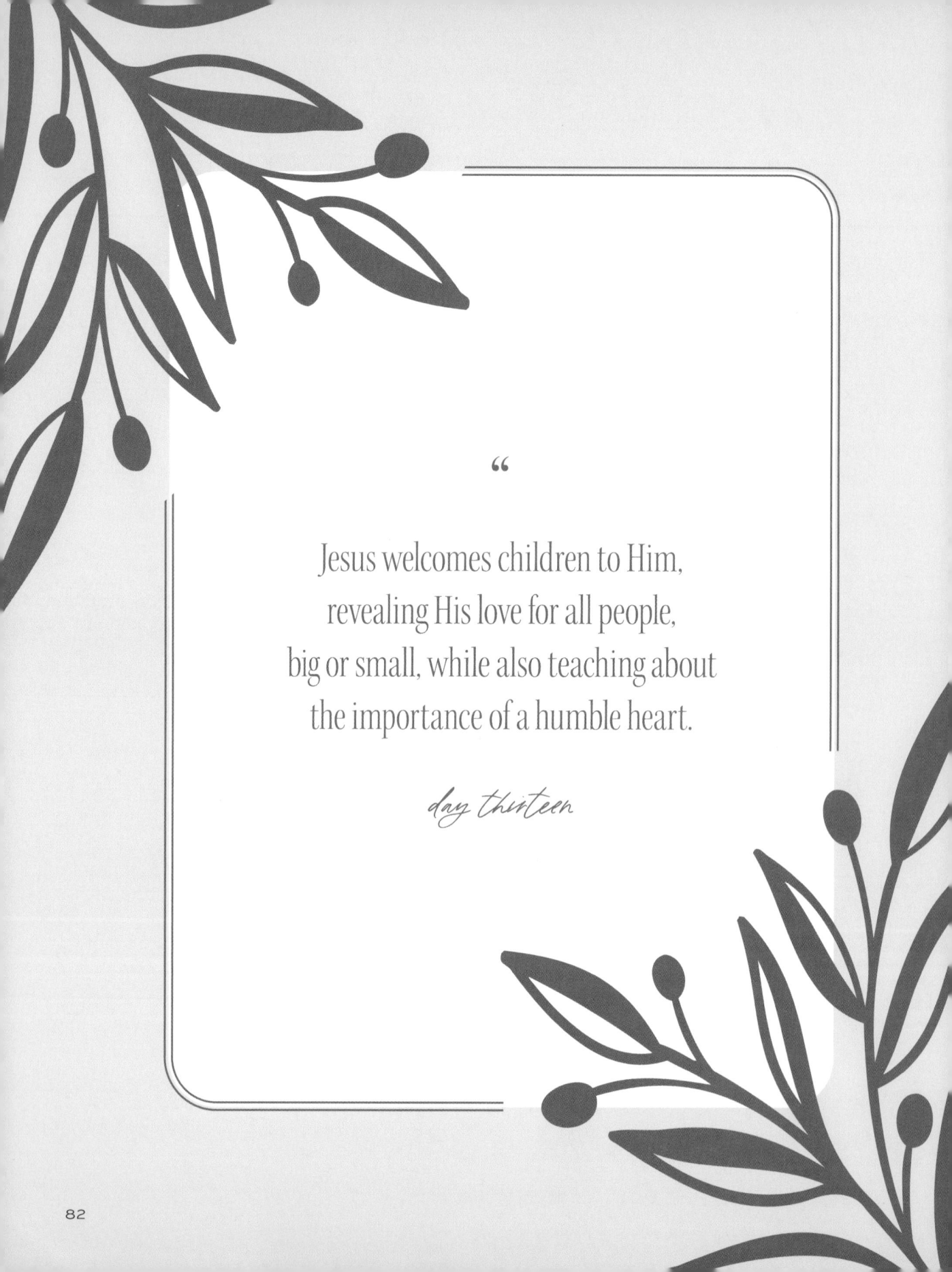

> Jesus welcomes children to Him,
> revealing His love for all people,
> big or small, while also teaching about
> the importance of a humble heart.

*day thirteen*

# Jesus and Children

READ MARK 10:13-16

One of the sweetest experiences for a parent is when their child runs into their arms. If a parent comes home from a trip or a long day at work, it can be such a joy to walk through the door, open their arms wide, and have their child come rushing in for an embrace. But could you imagine what it would be like for the child if their parent pushed them away? They would likely feel crushed to be rejected in such a way. This is not what Jesus does, however, and we see this to be true in Mark 10:13–16. In this passage, Jesus welcomes children to Him, revealing His love for all people, big or small, while also teaching about the importance of a humble heart.

Mark 10:13–16 describes a time when little children are being brought to Jesus. The disciples rebuke the people for bringing the children, revealing the disciples' lack of humility. They seemingly believe it is shameful for children to be brought to Jesus, perhaps because children were often viewed as insignificant in the ancient world. They might believe that only those who are well-known or elite should come to their great Teacher. But Jesus does not share these thoughts. Rather, He is angered by the disciples' actions and welcomes the children to Himself.

What follows is a beautiful picture of Christ's love as He takes the children in His arms. He does what the people desire by laying His hands on them, but He takes a step further by blessing them. How Jesus blessed the children, we do not know, but such action continues to reveal Jesus's love and ultimately points to God's love for those who are often cast out or overlooked.

As Jesus welcomes the children to Himself, He takes the moment to teach an important lesson about God's kingdom. He teaches that people must posture themselves like children in order to come into God's kingdom. Children are helpless without their parents or someone to care for them, so they look to them for help. They recognize their need for help and depend on their parents or those who take care of them to receive what they need. In the same way, to belong to God's kingdom, people must acknowledge their utter helplessness without Christ, look to Him, and trust in Him. The one who does not act like a little child is one who does not see their need for Jesus or denies their helplessness apart from Him. Those who respond this way will not receive God's kingdom, but those who posture themselves like a child will receive His kingdom.

While it may feel discouraging to admit our helplessness, we are all the more reminded of God's grace for us through Christ when we do. When we see our need and reach out our arms to our heavenly Father, He does not turn us away. Because of Christ's love and grace, we are welcomed and received by the Father, who holds us in His eternal embrace.

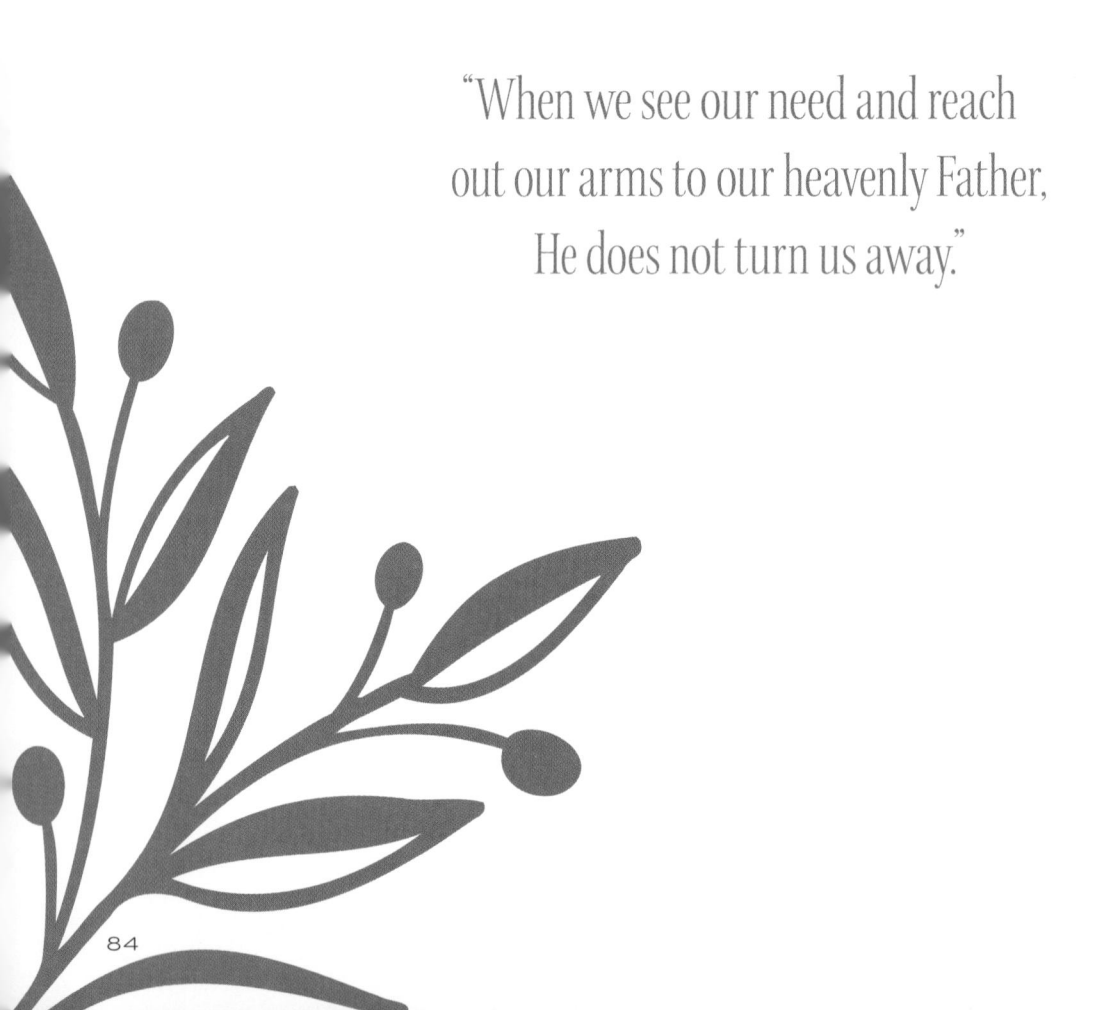

> "When we see our need and reach out our arms to our heavenly Father, He does not turn us away."

**REFLECT**

What does it look like for you to posture yourself as a child in your daily life? How would your dependence on the Lord change if you regularly postured yourself in this way?

**PRAY**

Thank God for the salvation that He gives you through Christ. Ask that God will help you acknowledge your need for Jesus regularly and come to Him in trust.

"
God's heart is for people from *all* nations — not just the Jews — to experience salvation.

*day fourteen*

# A House of Prayer

READ MATTHEW 21:12–13

"Do you have to do that *here*?"

Have you ever found yourself saying or at least thinking these words? Maybe a child is loudly playing with their toys—not in their own room but in yours—while you are trying to rest. Or someone is loudly talking on their phone in a quiet space instead of taking the call outside. Sometimes, a person's actions are situationally inappropriate, a point demonstrated by Jesus when He overturned the tables of the money changers in the temple courts. Through His actions, Jesus reiterates the truth that God's heart is for people from *all* nations—not just the Jews—to experience salvation.

It is important to note that the money changers and those selling animals for sacrifice were performing important and even necessary jobs. The temple tax, for example, could only be paid with a certain type of coin, one which Jews coming from all over the Roman Empire would not have had. And bringing sacrificial animals across such large distances, as some had to travel, was just not practical.

But it is *where* these people are conducting their business that bothers Jesus. Surrounding the temple were various areas (or "courts") beyond which certain groups could not go. The outermost court was the court of the Gentiles. For non-Jewish people who wanted to worship Israel's God, this was the space designated for them to do so. And yet it was here that the money changers were allowed by the priests to set up shop. Gentiles who came to pray thus had to do so over the noise of a crowded marketplace nearby.

This enrages Jesus, who overturns the tables and reminds them of the temple's purpose. He first quotes Isaiah 56:7, speaking of Gentiles coming to worship God at the temple, which will be "a house of prayer for all nations." But the religious leaders have fallen far short of this ideal and made the temple "a den of robbers," words taken from Jeremiah 7, in which Jeremiah strongly rebukes the people of Jerusalem for going through the motions of religious observance while flagrantly living in ways that displease God.

The *where* of the business the people were conducting did not have to be inside the temple courts. This business could have been (and previously was) conducted outside of it. By allowing it to happen in the court of the Gentiles, the temple authorities were not only disregarding the entire purpose of the temple but their calling as the people of Israel. As God's chosen people, Israel was called to bring God's blessing to all nations, not to hoard it for themselves.

Jesus's words and actions, then, demonstrate God's concern for all people. No one who seeks to worship Him should be prevented from doing so. And His words reinforce the point that those of us who have experienced God's grace should seek to extend that grace to others. Jesus's words are a challenge to make Him known to those around us.

> "Those of us who have experienced God's grace should seek to extend that grace to others."

**REFLECT**

Do you live with an eagerness to make Jesus known to others around you? In what ways are you tempted to treat your faith as private (i.e., just "me and Jesus")?

**PRAY**

Pray that God will increase your desire to see people from all nations come to faith in Jesus. Ask Him what role you can play in seeing the gospel go to those in unreached places.

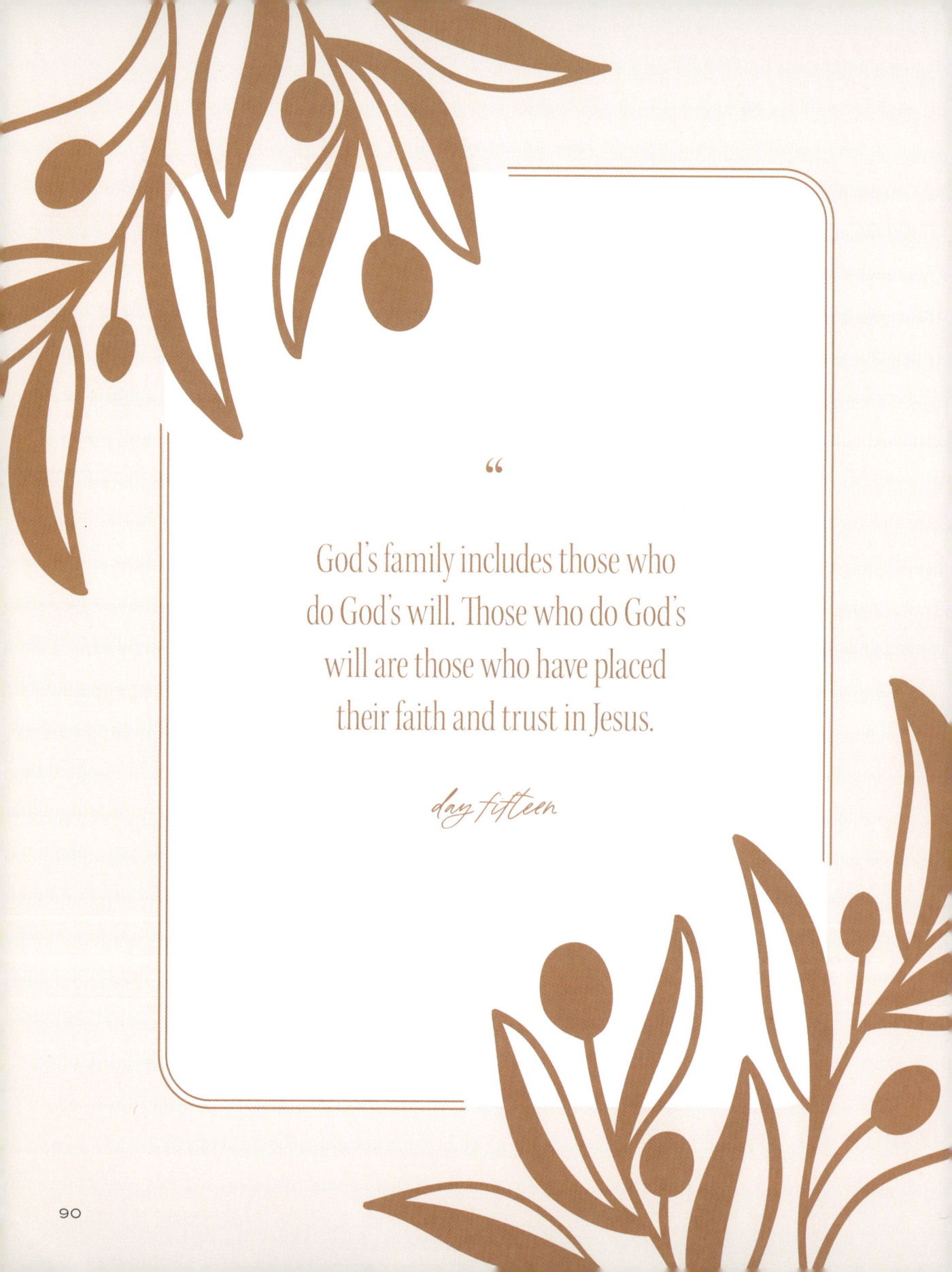

"

God's family includes those who do God's will. Those who do God's will are those who have placed their faith and trust in Jesus.

*day fifteen*

# Here Are My Mother, Brothers, and Sisters

READ MARK 3:31–35

Imagine a young man has just asked his girlfriend's parents for their blessing to marry their daughter. He tries to contain his nervousness as he looks at the parents and waits for their response. When the parents agree, he lets out a small sigh of relief, but he becomes anxious again when the father hands him a list of requirements. "In order for you to marry our daughter and join our family, you must do these things." The young man's heart sinks as he scans the list before him, wondering how he possibly can check off every last requirement.

It is possible for us to believe we have to earn God's favor or meet a list of requirements to be part of God's family. But thankfully, Scripture tells us otherwise. Belonging to God's family is a gift given to us by grace through faith in Christ. Jesus reminds us of this truth in Mark 3:31–35.

In the Gospel of Mark, Jesus teaches that there are insiders and outsiders to God's kingdom. Those who view themselves as "insiders" are often the religious elite, who believe their good works earn them a place in God's family. These people, in turn, believe that the "outsiders" are sinners, Gentiles, or any other person who falls outside the category of a law-abiding Jew. But Jesus turns this idea on the religious leaders' heads. He teaches how the outsiders are actually insiders, and the supposed "insiders" are really outsiders.

Jesus's words in today's passage are not meant to snub His family but rather to speak to a greater reality—that God's family includes those who do God's will. Those who do God's will are those who have placed their faith and trust in Jesus. They are those currently sitting at Jesus's feet in Mark 3:31–35, eagerly listening to and believing Jesus's teachings. Jesus's words reveal that it is not those who have a certain pedigree who belong to God's family. Nor is it those who obey the whole Law. Rather, God's family consists of followers of Jesus who do the will of the Father. Doing God's will involves worshiping and glorifying God and loving others in obedience to God.

Such teaching from Jesus comforts those of us who feel too far from God or unworthy to be His disciples. His words wash relief over those of us who believe that we must perform perfectly to be called a child of God. We do nothing of our own merit to earn entrance into God's family. All we must do is receive the free gift of salvation that Jesus gives us by grace and through faith. When we receive this gift, we are called God's children and are brought into His eternal family (John 1:12–13). And for the rest of our days, we get to do the will of the One who has welcomed us into His family through Christ.

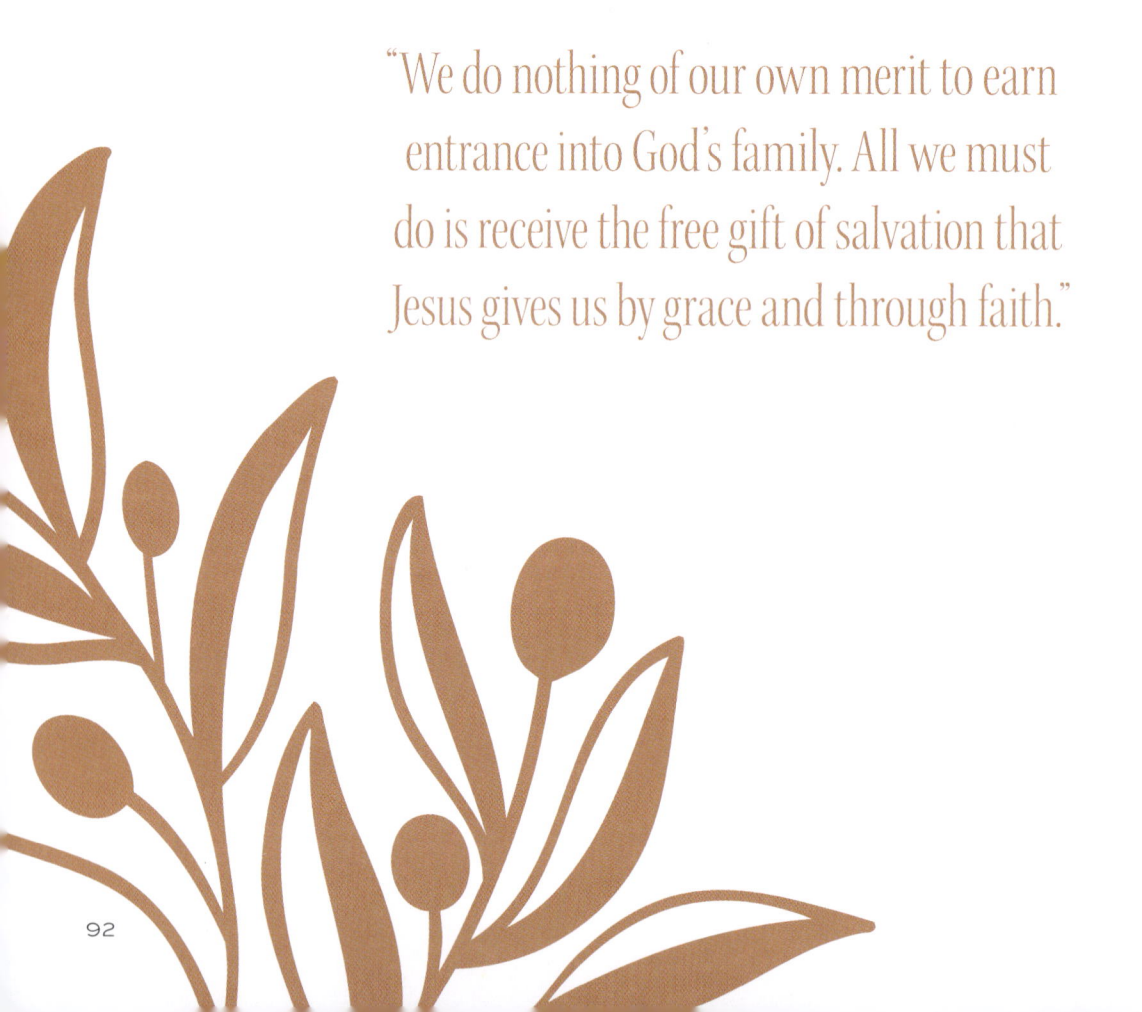

> "We do nothing of our own merit to earn entrance into God's family. All we must do is receive the free gift of salvation that Jesus gives us by grace and through faith."

**REFLECT**

How have you been trying to earn or maintain a status in God's family? How does today's passage encourage you to rest in Christ's grace and the position He gives you in God's family?

**PRAY**

Thank God for allowing you to be part of His family through Christ and ask that, in response, you will continually seek to do God's will.

"

Jesus's heart is to seek and save the lost, no matter how lost one might be.

*day sixteen*

# Zacchaeus

READ LUKE 19:1–10

Some of us may believe we are too sinful to be forgiven. Perhaps we feel that our past is too tainted, the list of our mistakes too long. Such beliefs can cause us to assume that only those who are "good" are worthy of Christ's salvation. So we hang our heads in shame and refuse to come to the One we think turns His face away from us. Luke 19:1–9 brings good news to those of us who feel like our sins are too insurmountable for Christ's grace. In this passage, we learn that Jesus's heart is to seek and save the lost, no matter how lost one might be.

Luke 19:1–9 tells the story of Jesus's interaction with a man named Zacchaeus. Luke tells us that Zacchaeus is a rich "chief tax collector" (verse 2). During Jesus's time, tax collectors were tasked with collecting money for Rome. They were typically looked down upon, as some would charge people more than necessary and then keep the extra for themselves. From Zacchaeus's own words, it seems that he, too, extorted people in this way—and him being a *chief* tax collector would have caused him to be held in great contempt, evidenced from the people's reaction to him in verse 7.

Even though Luke tells us that Zacchaeus is sinful, he desires to see Jesus, so much so that he scrambles up a tree to catch a glimpse of Him. While Luke says that Jesus is just passing through Jericho (verse 1), Jesus takes the time to notice Zacchaeus and call him down from the tree. Not only this, but Jesus desires to stay in Zacchaeus's home, stating that it is "necessary" for Him to do so (verse 5). Zacchaeus welcomes Jesus joyfully, but the crowd scoffs, wondering why Jesus is staying with someone so sinful. Jesus responds differently by proclaiming Zacchaeus's salvation, despite Zacchaeus's sin. Jesus has come to seek and save the lost, and Zacchaeus is among those whom He has saved.

Zacchaeus's story reminds us that no one is too sinful to receive Christ's salvation. Grace and forgiveness are available for us in Jesus Christ no matter the wrong we have done. And when we repent and receive the salvation Jesus offers us, we are changed. As we see in Zacchaeus's story, Jesus's response to Zacchaeus and the salvation He gives him caused Zacchaeus to change his ways (verse 8). Jesus sees sinners, seeks sinners, and saves sinners. Because of Jesus's heart toward sinners and the sacrifice on the cross that He made for them, we are forgiven and changed from the inside out.

> "Jesus sees sinners, seeks sinners, and saves sinners."

REFLECT

In what ways does Christ's desire to seek and save the lost humble you?

PRAY

Thank Jesus for the salvation that He so graciously offers, and praise Him for the ways you have seen His salvation change your life.

*week 3 conclusion*

Jesus sees those who are often unseen by the world. He calls blessed those whom the world might call unfortunate. He welcomes into His family and gives rest to all who come to Him. As we conclude this week, give thanks to Jesus for opening His arms to you. Pray that you would see yourself not through the eyes of the world, or even your own, but through God's eyes.

> "Jesus sees those who are often unseen by the world."

week 4

# Words about Our Relationship with God

## memory verse

He said to him, "Love the Lord your God with all your heart, with all your soul, and with all your mind. This is the greatest and most important command."

MATTHEW 22:37-38

## introduction

Over the next two weeks, we will look at what Jesus has to say about our relationships, both with God and with others. The first day of this week will introduce the next two weeks with a saying in which Jesus demonstrates how intertwined these two sets of relationships are. The rest of this week will look specifically at our relationship with God. Who is He to us? Who are we to Him? And how should the answers to these questions affect our daily lives?

"
We must love God with our whole selves — with the totality of our being.

*day seventeen*

# The Greatest Commandment

READ MATTHEW 22:37-40

Have you ever been overwhelmed with an endless to-do list? Looking at it, you wonder how you will possibly have the time to do everything. In these moments, you might end up prioritizing the items on the list and considering what *must* be completed versus what you would *like* to complete. You ask, *What task—if accomplished—would make this day a win?* In a similar way, when Jesus was asked what the most important commandment was (and there were many!), He distilled all of God's commands down to love—love for God and love for others.

In Matthew 22:34–36, Jesus is tested by an expert in the Law who asks Him what the greatest command in the Law is. Many teachers had identified 613 distinct commands throughout the Torah (Genesis through Deuteronomy in the Bible), and while all were important, the presence of so many commands led to questions of the relative importance of each. But people disagreed over how to rank them, and by presenting this question to Jesus, this man likely figures that however Jesus answers, He is sure to alienate someone. It is all an attempt to discredit Him.

But Jesus cuts to the core of all God's commands with His answer. The "greatest and most important command," He says, is to "Love the Lord your God with all your heart, with all your soul, and with all your mind" (Matthew 22:37–38). Jesus is quoting from Deuteronomy 6:5, which was part of the central confession of the Jewish people (Deuteronomy 6:4–9), and many would have recited these words twice a day. At the center of what God requires of His people is that they would love Him. In speaking of our "heart," "soul," and "strength," Jesus is not speaking of three distinct components within us; rather, He is saying that we must love God with our whole selves—with the totality of our being.

But Jesus goes beyond the question asked and speaks of a "second" command that "is like it: Love your neighbor as yourself" (from Leviticus 19:18). This is a natural extension of the first, for if we love God, we will love what is important to Him: human beings made in His image. Love for God, then, will be seen in how we treat others. And loving others is an important aspect of loving God. These two loves are intertwined, a point often made in Scripture (Matthew 7:12, Romans 13:8–10, Galatians 5:14, James 1:27, 1 John 4:7–10).

On these two commands, all "the Law and the Prophets depend" (Matthew 22:40). Love, therefore, ought to be the cumulative effect of obeying God's commands. And it should mark our lives as followers of Jesus (John 15:12).

> "If we love God, we will love what is important to Him: human beings made in His image."

**REFLECT**

Why is love for God and others so important when it comes to living out the various commands found in the Bible? What happens when we obey the Bible's commands but do so without love?

**PRAY**

Pray that God would deepen your love for Him, and ask that He would reveal to you ways that you can demonstrate love to others.

"

We wait with eager expectation for Jesus to return and wipe away every last trace of sin and its effects.

*day eighteen*

# The Lord's Prayer

READ MATTHEW 6:9–13

To a large degree, how we address other people is shaped by our relationship with them. A parent may address their fussy toddler as "Grumpy Pants" but (hopefully!) not a close peer who is upset. A wife and husband may use terms of endearment for each other that they would not use for anyone else. And we probably speak to friends in ways we would not speak to a supervisor at work. Similarly, Jesus teaches us that how we address God ought to be shaped by the reality that He is our Father.

Well-known by many, what is often called the Lord's Prayer is found in Matthew 6:9–13. To appreciate this prayer, it is worth considering the verses leading up to it, in which Jesus first addresses how *not* to pray. Our prayers, He says, should not be performative, a way to make others see how "holy" we are (verses 5–6). Nor should they be overly wordy, as if only longer prayers will get God's attention (verses 7–8). For Jesus's followers to pray in such ways is to ignore a critical dimension of prayer, namely that God is our Father. Our prayers should "Therefore" (verse 9) be shaped by an awareness of this relationship.

The Lord's Prayer is a model of just such a prayer. It begins with an acknowledgment that God is "Our Father in heaven." The term used for "Father"—*abba*—is an intimate one used by children to address their fathers. That Jesus instructs us to use it in prayer speaks to the privilege it is to have such intimacy with God (Romans 8:15, Galatians 4:6).

It is significant to note that this prayer begins with an acknowledgment of who God is and with requests for His purposes to advance. It is all too easy to jump into prayer and immediately begin telling God what we need. But this prayer begins with requests that God's name would be "honored as holy," that His "kingdom [would] come" and

His "will be done on earth as it is in heaven" (verses 9–10). In prayer, we should ask that God's holiness would be acknowledged, that the gospel would spread, and that our lives would conform to His will.

Only then does the prayer move to our own needs. Jesus instructs us to ask our Father to provide the necessities of life, to forgive us our sins, and to protect us from giving in to temptations to sin. And since God is our Father, these are things that He delights to give us.

Jesus's point in offering this prayer was not necessarily that we must pray these words verbatim (though we certainly can!). Rather, it is a framework of what our prayers should look like. In prayer, we should acknowledge God as our Father, pray for His name to be honored and known in the world, and then ask our Father to provide what we need.

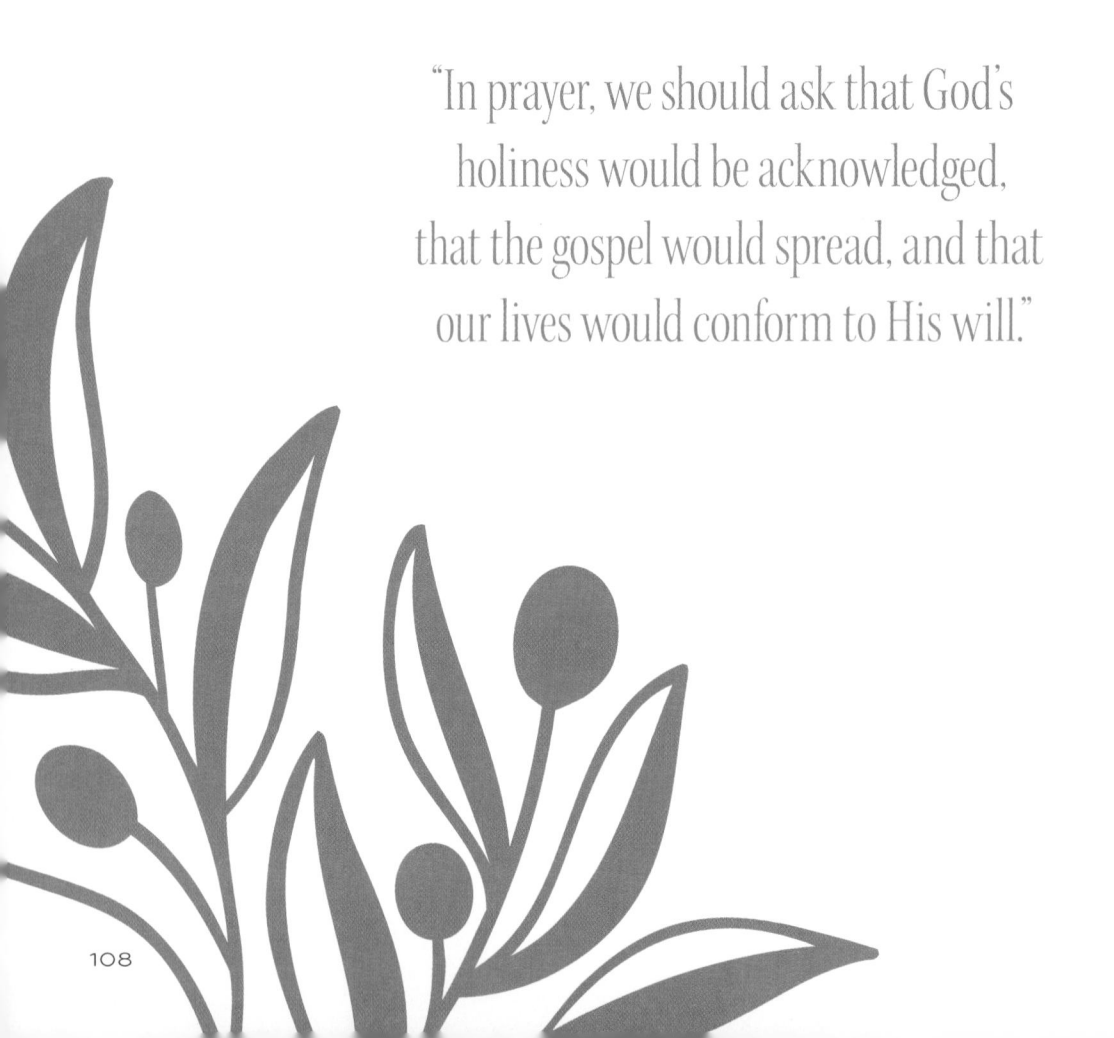

> "In prayer, we should ask that God's holiness would be acknowledged, that the gospel would spread, and that our lives would conform to His will."

## REFLECT

How does acknowledging God as Father affect how we approach Him? How can remembering that He is a loving, attentive Father encourage you in your prayer life?

## PRAY

Take some time to pray the Lord's Prayer, printed below, either verbatim or in your own words.

### The Lord's Prayer (Matthew 6:9b–13)

*Our Father in heaven,*
*your name be honored as holy.*
*Your kingdom come.*
*Your will be done*
*on earth as it is in heaven.*
*Give us today our daily bread.*
*And forgive us our debts,*
*as we also have forgiven our debtors.*
*And do not bring us into temptation,*
*but deliver us from the evil one.*

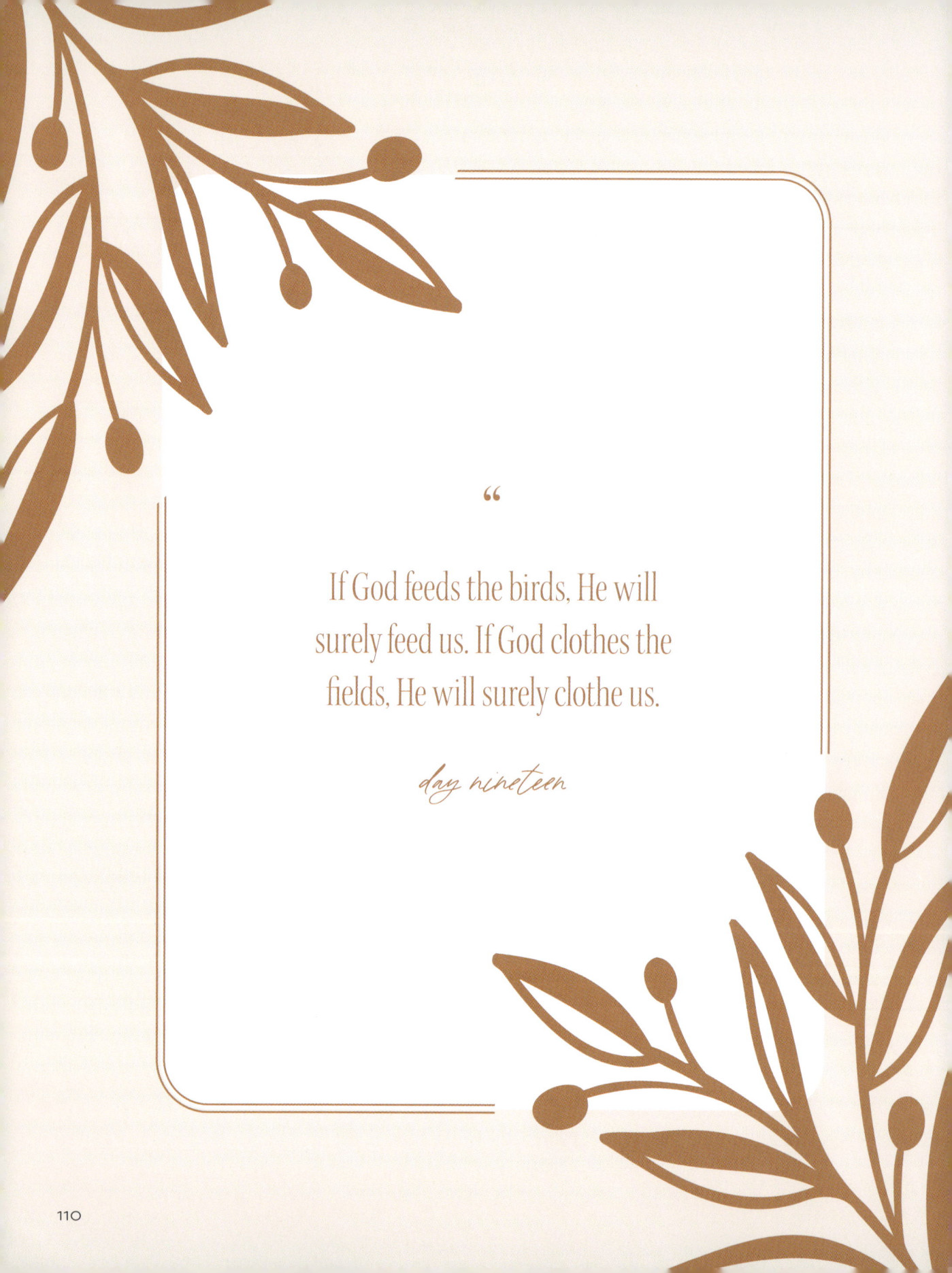

> If God feeds the birds, He will surely feed us. If God clothes the fields, He will surely clothe us.

*day nineteen*

# Don't Worry

READ LUKE 12:22–30

There always seems to be something to worry about in our lives. We worry whether we have enough money in our bank accounts. We worry whether we have enough food to feed ourselves or our families. We worry whether we will remain healthy or what we would do if we were to become seriously sick. While the brokenness of this world and the troubles that come with it are difficult, they do not have to leave us anxious. In Luke 12:22–30, Jesus calls us to not worry by reminding us of the consistent care of our heavenly Father.

If we read Luke 12:22 on its own, listening to Jesus's words might be hard. After all, it is not easy to simply stop worrying over the cares in our lives. How can we not worry when the bills keep stacking up, when our child must be hospitalized, or when we cannot find work to provide for ourselves or our family? Jesus gives us the answer in the verses that follow verse 22. If God feeds the birds, He will surely feed us. If God clothes the fields, He will surely clothe us. These words are not a promise that God will keep us from all troubles. Nor do they promise that God will answer every need of provision in the way we desire. Rather, these words promise us that our God cares for us and provides for us, and because He does, we do not need to worry.

Instead of becoming anxious over our needs, we can rest in the truth that our heavenly Father knows what we need. Our troubles are not hidden from His sight. He is not blind to the needs that must be met. In His perfect love and sovereignty, God sees our cares and provides for us. If we doubt this truth, we need only look to the birds in the sky and the lilies of the field to be reminded that if God takes care of the birds and the flowers, He will certainly take care of us, His children.

The gospel also reminds us of God's provision. While God provides for our daily needs, He has already provided for our greatest need through Christ. Because of Jesus's death and resurrection, we are able to experience forgiveness and eternal life. Therefore, the physical ways that God provides for us ultimately point to the spiritual provision He has given us through Christ.

When we consider and rest in the truth of God's provision and care, we are able to listen to Jesus's words instructing us not to worry. We are able to hold our needs loosely, trusting that God will do something about them in His perfect sovereignty and timing. Rather than fixing our eyes on our troubles, we are able to fix our eyes on our heavenly Father, who never stops caring for us.

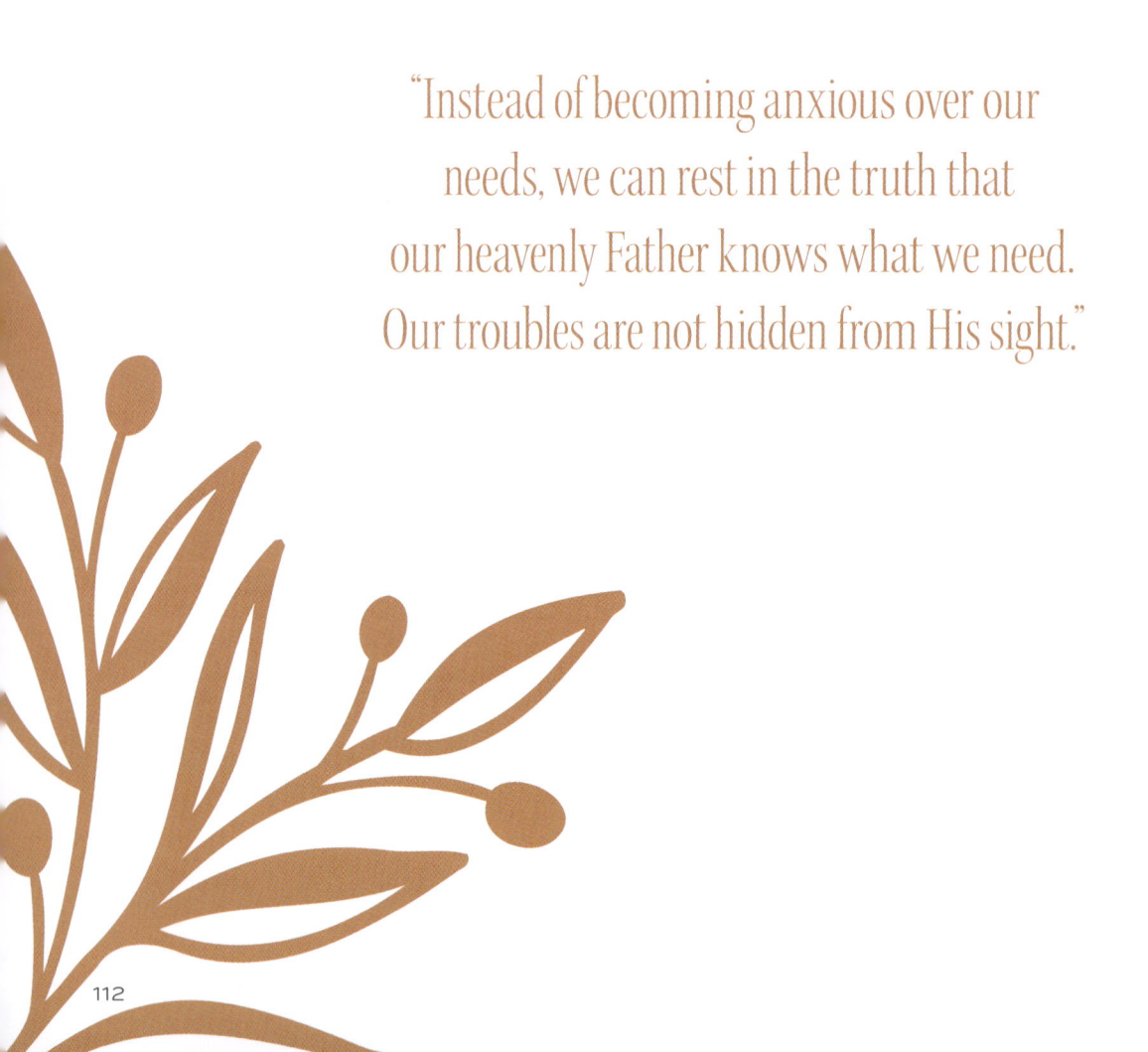

> "Instead of becoming anxious over our needs, we can rest in the truth that our heavenly Father knows what we need. Our troubles are not hidden from His sight."

**REFLECT**

How are you prone to worry? How does God's care for you bring comfort in your worries?

**PRAY**

Thank God for His constant care for you and ask Him to help you not worry and instead trust in His care and provision.

"

Jesus demonstrates that our ultimate allegiance must be to God.

*day twenty*

# Give to God What Is God's

READ MARK 12:17

Have you ever seen a sign or bumper sticker that says something like "A House Divided"? These are often accompanied by the logos of two rival sports teams or colleges. It is a humorous picture of how allegiances sometimes come into conflict. *I am devoted to my family, yes, but I am also devoted to seeing my team crush yours!* In Mark 12, Jesus is tested with a question about competing allegiance. And in His response, Jesus demonstrates that our ultimate allegiance must be to God.

In Mark 12:13, Jesus's opponents set out to "trap him in his words." After first flattering Jesus, they lay the trap, asking whether or not it is lawful to pay taxes to Caesar. It is a clever move on their part. They figure that if Jesus says, *Yes, it is lawful*, the crowds who adore Him will turn on Him. And if Jesus says, *No, it is not lawful*, they can then inform the Roman authorities that He is a rebel and let them deal with Jesus. In their minds, they have cornered Jesus.

Jesus then takes a coin and asks whose "image and inscription" is on it (Mark 12:16). The answer, obvious to His audience, is Caesar. So Jesus instructs them to pay the tax. Since the coin bears the image of Caesar, the money ought to be given back to him.

But Jesus does not stop there. Had He done so, He might have been labeled as being "pro-Rome." Rather, Jesus rejects the question's assumption that *either* you worship God *or* you pay taxes to Rome. Both can be true. Give to Caesar what belongs to him, Jesus explains, and give to God what belongs to Him. Caesar does have some claims on them, but they pale in comparison to God's claims on them. Divine rights belong to God alone.

Jesus may also be echoing Genesis 1 in His response. That is, just as Caesar has a right to that which bears his image, so too does God have a right to what bears His. But what bears God's image? Human beings (Genesis 1:26–27). It is as if Jesus is saying, *Caesar can have your coins, but give your whole self to God.*

Jesus's words here remind us that though our lives are filled with many responsibilities, both to people and institutions, our primary allegiance is to God. In fact, fulfilling these various responsibilities is a way to demonstrate this primary allegiance. We can worship God by paying our taxes (Romans 13:1–7) and by caring for others (1 John 3:17–18). May God's claim on our entire being, therefore, cause us to see everything we do as an opportunity to serve Him.

> "Though our lives are filled with many responsibilities, both to people and institutions, our primary allegiance is to God."

**REFLECT**

How can remembering God's claim on your entire life impact the way you go about your everyday tasks? How can it transform your approach to tasks that you do not particularly enjoy?

**PRAY**

Pray that God would help you to prioritize your allegiance to Him above all other allegiances.

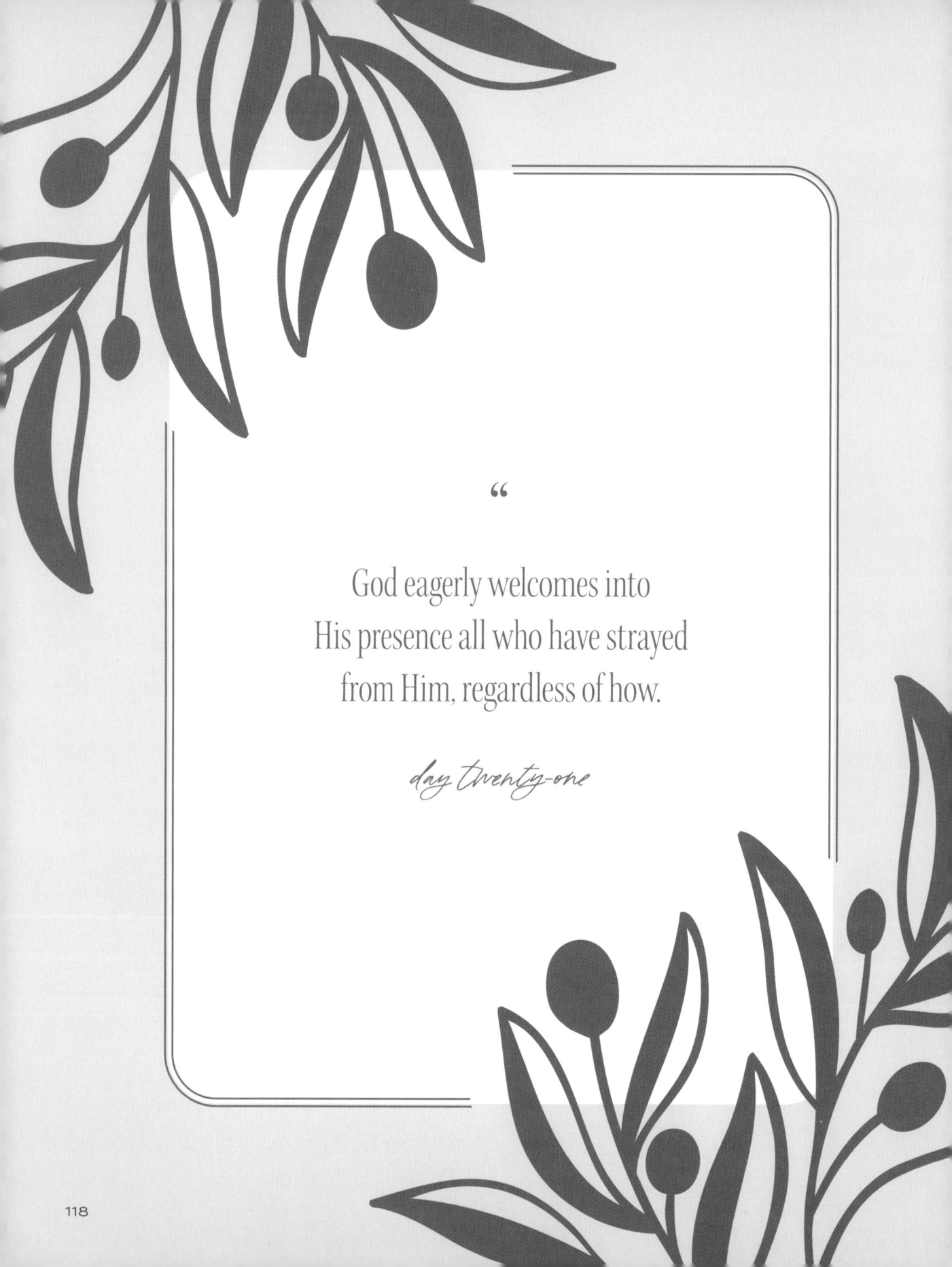

"
God eagerly welcomes into
His presence all who have strayed
from Him, regardless of how.

*day twenty-one*

# The Lost Son(s)

READ LUKE 15:11–32

According to the Bible, all have sinned and deserve God's wrath. Some people's sins might be visible, while others' might be more subtle, hidden behind an "upright" or "holy" veneer. Both types of people need God's grace, and in Luke 15, Jesus reminds us that God eagerly welcomes into His presence all who have strayed from Him, regardless of how.

In Luke 15:1–2, the Pharisees and scribes criticize Jesus for welcoming tax collectors and sinners. Jesus responds with three parables, each involving something lost being found. First, a man finds a lost sheep (verses 3–7). Second, a woman finds a lost coin (verses 8–10). Both rejoice over finding what was lost, and each parable closes with Jesus's comment that there is likewise rejoicing in heaven when sinners repent (Luke 15:7, 10).

In the third parable, we meet a man with two sons, the younger of whom asks his father for his inheritance. Since an inheritance would typically only be given upon a father's death (Numbers 27:8–11), it is as if the son is telling his father that he wishes he were dead. And by leaving, this son is neglecting to honor his father (Exodus 20:12).

But after squandering his wealth and experiencing famine, this son plans to humble himself and beg to be one of his father's servants, having forfeited all rights to be his father's son. Yet he vastly underestimates the love of his father, who does not even let his son finish his "I'm sorry" speech before preparing to fully restore him and celebrate his return. This father embodies the kind of rejoicing that Jesus has spoken of in the previous two parables (Luke 15:7, 10).

But the older brother is enraged. Notice his language: he sees his loving father as a slave master (Luke 15:29). He refers to his brother as "this son of yours" (Luke 15:30). Though the lost son has been found, another son is now in danger of straying. He has forgotten the privilege and joy it is to be his father's son and views their relationship as transactional: *I do good work, and you reward me.* He, too, has strayed from his father, though he never physically left home. Through this older brother, Jesus rebukes the Pharisees who refuse to rejoice over the tax collectors and sinners coming to Jesus and invites them to share in His celebration.

This parable thus offers comfort and a warning. The older brother is a warning for when we are tempted to look down on others who seem like worse sinners than we are. It forces us to ask ourselves how we see God—as our Father? Or as a slave master? And for those of us who find ourselves far off like the younger brother, Jesus in this parable offers the comforting reminder that God is a Father whose arms are always open. Whether our straying has been visible or subtle, God rejoices when we come to Him.

> "God is a Father whose arms are always open. Whether our straying has been visible or subtle, God rejoices when we come to Him."

**REFLECT**

How did each son's view of his father impact their actions in this parable? How might a greater awareness of God being your Father impact your own actions?

**PRAY**

Give thanks to God for welcoming you into His arms when you, too, were lost. Pray that you would always cherish the privilege this relationship is and rejoice when others find salvation in Jesus.

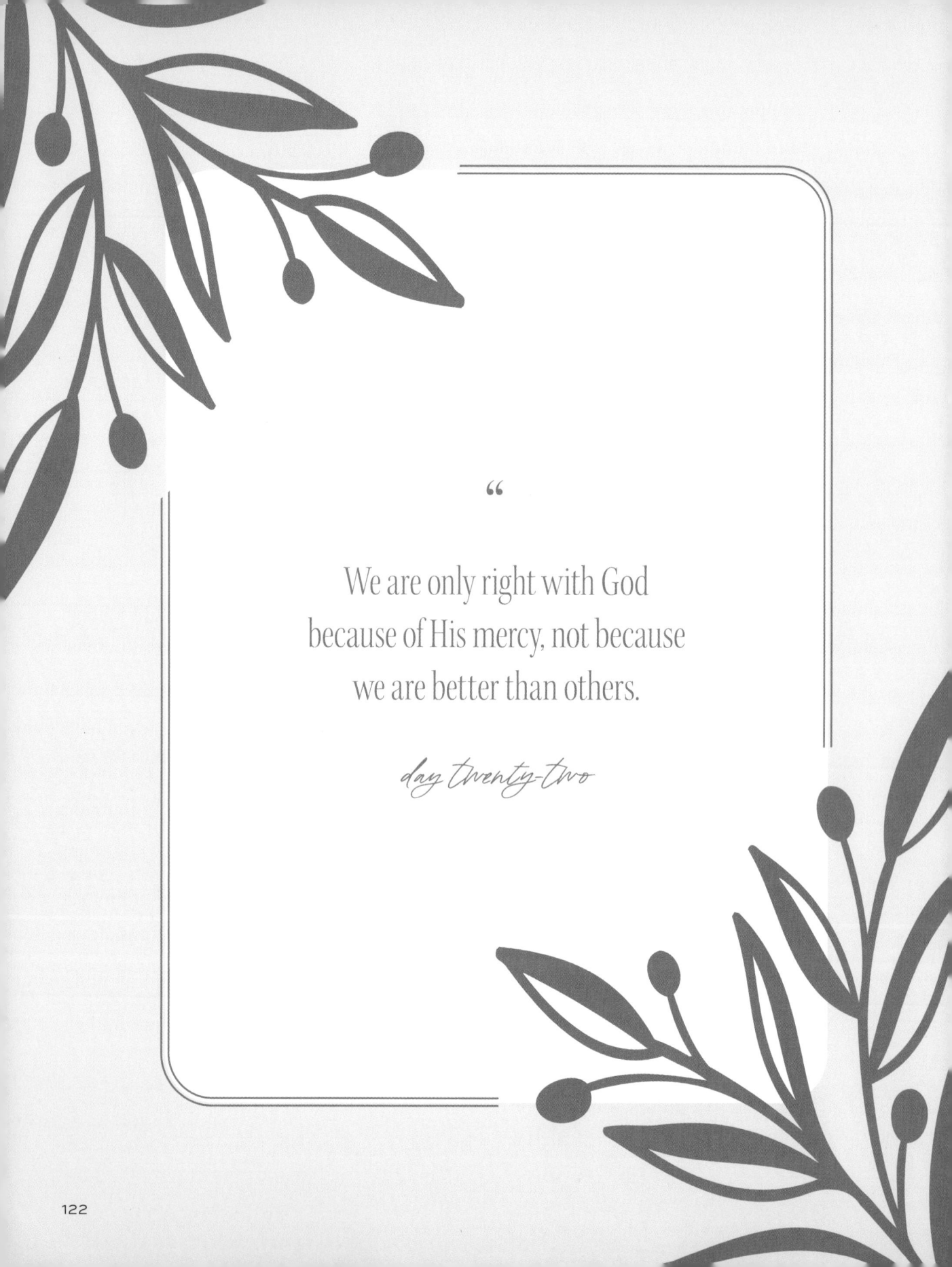

> "
> We are only right with God because of His mercy, not because we are better than others.

*day twenty-two*

# The Pharisee and the Tax Collector

READ LUKE 18:9–14

Have you ever known someone who acted "holier than thou"? Someone who saw themselves as morally superior to others and looked down on them? We dislike such people, but if we are honest, sometimes we *are* those people. Even in subtle ways, we can measure others against how we live as a way to feel better about ourselves. This attitude resides in all of us, and to this attitude, Jesus reminds us that we are only right with God because of His mercy, not because we are better than others.

This is memorably demonstrated in Jesus's parable about a Pharisee and a tax collector. Luke explicitly tells us that Jesus directed this parable to those "who trusted in themselves that they were righteous and looked down on everyone else" (Luke 18:9). Though Luke does not specifically mention Pharisees here, the parable itself leads us to conclude that this is precisely the group that Jesus is targeting.

In the parable, two men go to the temple to pray. The Pharisee's presence there is natural. He is, in the eyes of many, a model of what devotion to God looks like. The tax collector's presence, however, might raise some eyebrows. As employees of the Roman Empire, tax collectors were despised by the Jews. And since they were Jews themselves, they were seen as traitors, Jews who profited from the oppression of their fellow Jews. The contrast between these two men is great.

But the contrast between their prayers is great as well. We might paraphrase the Pharisee's prayer as: *God, I thank You . . . for me!* He starts out strong by giving thanks to God. But he does not mention God again. The Pharisee's focus is on himself. He thanks God that he is not a notorious sinner like the tax collector (verse 11). And he boasts, not just of how he has obeyed the Law but how he has gone beyond its requirements (verse 12).

The tax collector's prayer, however, could not be more different. Conscious of his sin and possibly surrounded in the temple by Jews who did not want him there, he is in anguish. While beating his breast (a sign of repentance) and unable to even look up to heaven, the man prays a desperate and simple prayer: "God, have mercy on me, a sinner!" (Luke 18:13). And it was *this* man, Jesus says, who went home justified, "because everyone who exalts himself will be humbled, but the one who humbles himself will be exalted" (Luke 18:14).

The tax collector sees clearly what the Pharisee—blinded by his pride—does not: that we are sinners who deserve God's just judgment. A sinner's relationship with God is marked by humility on our end and mercy on God's. Being "justified"—or made right with God—is therefore not an achievement we earn; it is a gift of God's mercy. This parable ought to humble us by reminding us that we have access to God, not because we are better than others but because of the mercy He has on us.

> "A sinner's relationship with God is marked by humility on our end and mercy on God's."

**REFLECT**

In what ways, even subtly, do you find yourself looking down on others (either because of what you do that they do not, or vice versa)? How should this parable impact how you approach God in prayer?

**PRAY**

Spend time thanking God for the mercy He has shown you. Ask Him to help you remember that your acceptance from Him is a gift and not an achievement you have earned.

## week 4 conclusion

Who are we to God? We are His creatures, made in His image to reflect Him. But we are also sinners. We have run from God and are lost. We are like the tax collector who knows how undeserving he is to even address God. But who is God to us? Through Jesus's life, death, and resurrection, we are God's children. He is our Father who wants us to bring our requests to Him — a caring Father who calls us not to worry, a joyful Father who eagerly embraces us. As we close out this week, take a few moments to dwell on the ways God has shown His love to you.

> Through Jesus's life, death, and resurrection, we are God's children.

*week 5*

# Words about Our Relationship with Others

## memory verse

Therefore, whatever you want others to do for you,
do also the same for them, for this is the Law and the Prophets.

MATTHEW 7:12

## introduction

Last week, we studied how God has shown His love to us. This week, our focus will shift slightly to the ways we are to show love to others. But God's love for us will remain in view throughout this week because how we live in relationship with others is deeply affected by our relationship with God. God calls us to treat others the way that He has treated us, so as you read this week's entries, remember that how Jesus calls us to live in relationship with others is a reflection of how God has related to us.

"

We are to love our enemies,
for in doing so,
we reflect God's own love.

*day twenty-three*

# Love Your Enemies

READ LUKE 6:27-28

What is something hard you have done? Maybe it was training for and running a marathon. Maybe it was learning a musical instrument or getting a degree. Maybe one of the hardest things you have done revolves around a season of life, like parenting young children. Life is full of tremendously challenging tasks, and Jesus's command to love our enemies would certainly be among them. Few things come less naturally to us, yet we are to love our enemies, for in doing so, we reflect God's own love.

In Luke 6:22, Jesus pronounces a blessing on those who are persecuted "because of the Son of Man." Jesus is acknowledging that following Him will involve making some enemies along the way. And in verses 27 and 28, He instructs us on how we are to treat those enemies. We are to love them, and He says to do good to them, bless them, and pray for them.

What is striking about Jesus's commands is how concerned the commands are with the well-being of our enemies. Loving our enemies certainly carries a *negative* component. That is, when insulted, we are not to retaliate (verse 29). But this love also carries a positive, highly demanding component. It involves seeking ways to practically do good to our enemies. It involves speaking well both to and about them. And it involves actively praying for God to do good to them. Jesus is calling us to practically seek out ways to contribute to the well-being of those who care nothing for our own.

This love is difficult, highly inconvenient, and again, it does not come naturally to us. We would often much rather pursue the well-being of our family members and friends. Yet as Jesus goes on to point out in Luke 6:32–34, everyone does this! Even sinners love those who love them. And they are more than willing to give away their possessions when they expect to be repaid. People are more than ready to love others when it serves their own interests or when it costs them nothing. But to actively pursue the good of those who pursue our harm? Giving without thought of repayment? That is another kind of love entirely.

This other kind of love is *God's* love, to be exact. Maybe you have heard the sayings, "Like father, like son," or "The apple doesn't fall far from the tree." The idea is that children resemble their parents, a point Jesus makes in Luke 6:35–36. We are to love our enemies and pursue their good because that is what God, our Father, does. In Romans 5:8, Paul writes that "God proves his own love for us in that while we were still sinners, Christ died for us." As beneficiaries of this kind of love that Jesus is describing in this passage, may we extend that same love to our enemies and pray that they, too, may come to know God as Father.

> "Jesus is calling us to practically seek out ways to contribute to the well-being of those who care nothing for our own."

**REFLECT**

What specific people in your life might God be calling you to extend this kind of love to? What are some practical ways that you can love them?

**PRAY**

Ask God to remind you of how He loved *you* while you were His enemy. Then, ask Him for the strength to show this same love to others.

"
There should be no limit
to our forgiveness.

*day twenty-four*

# Forgiving Others

READ MATTHEW 18:21-35

We all mess up—sometimes in big ways. We make mistakes, we say the wrong thing, we hurt people's feelings. If we are fortunate, people might give us a second chance. If we are really fortunate, we might get a *second* second chance. Yet, at a certain point, people's patience often begins to wear thin, and the number of chances runs out. However, as followers of Jesus, we should live lives characterized by the forgiveness that Christ has shown us in His great grace.

In Matthew 18:21, Peter asks Jesus, "how many times should I forgive a brother or sister who sins against me? As many as seven times?" Commentator Leon Morris helpfully points out that there "was a rabbinic view that one need forgive only three times. . . . Peter more than doubled this quota of forgiveness" (471). Peter, therefore, probably feels like he is being merciful in his suggestion. By replying, *Not seven, but seventy times seven*, Jesus is not correcting Peter's number but his mindset. In effect, Jesus is saying, *If you are counting, you are missing the point*. There should be no limit to our forgiveness.

Jesus illustrates this concept with a parable about a king who graciously pardons the debt of a servant who owes him a lot of money. When this servant encounters a fellow servant who owes him a much smaller amount, the servant fails to imitate the king's generosity and instead throws his fellow servant in prison. The parable's point is simple: because God has forgiven us, we are to forgive others.

But the parable's point is considerably amplified by its details. The unmerciful servant owes the king "ten thousand talents" (Matthew 18:24). A talent itself was a substantial amount of money. And he owes ten *thousand* of them. It is hard to exaggerate the amount of money this man owes. This debt is staggering and not in several lifetimes could he ever repay it. By contrast, the debt that this servant was unwilling to forgive—while still a substantial amount—was a mere fraction of what he had been forgiven.

It is not easy to forgive others. As with loving our enemies, forgiving even fellow believers ranks among the most difficult things we are called to do as Christians. Jesus's point here is not to minimize the pain that others cause us but to put it into perspective. We owed an unpayable debt to God because of our sin, and God in His mercy absorbed that debt at great cost to Himself: the life of His own Son (see Romans 8:32). When we consider God's forgiveness, it is unthinkable for us to withhold it from others. He has forgiven far more in us than He asks us to forgive in others. Because of this, our lives should be marked not by bitterness and resentment but by forgiveness.

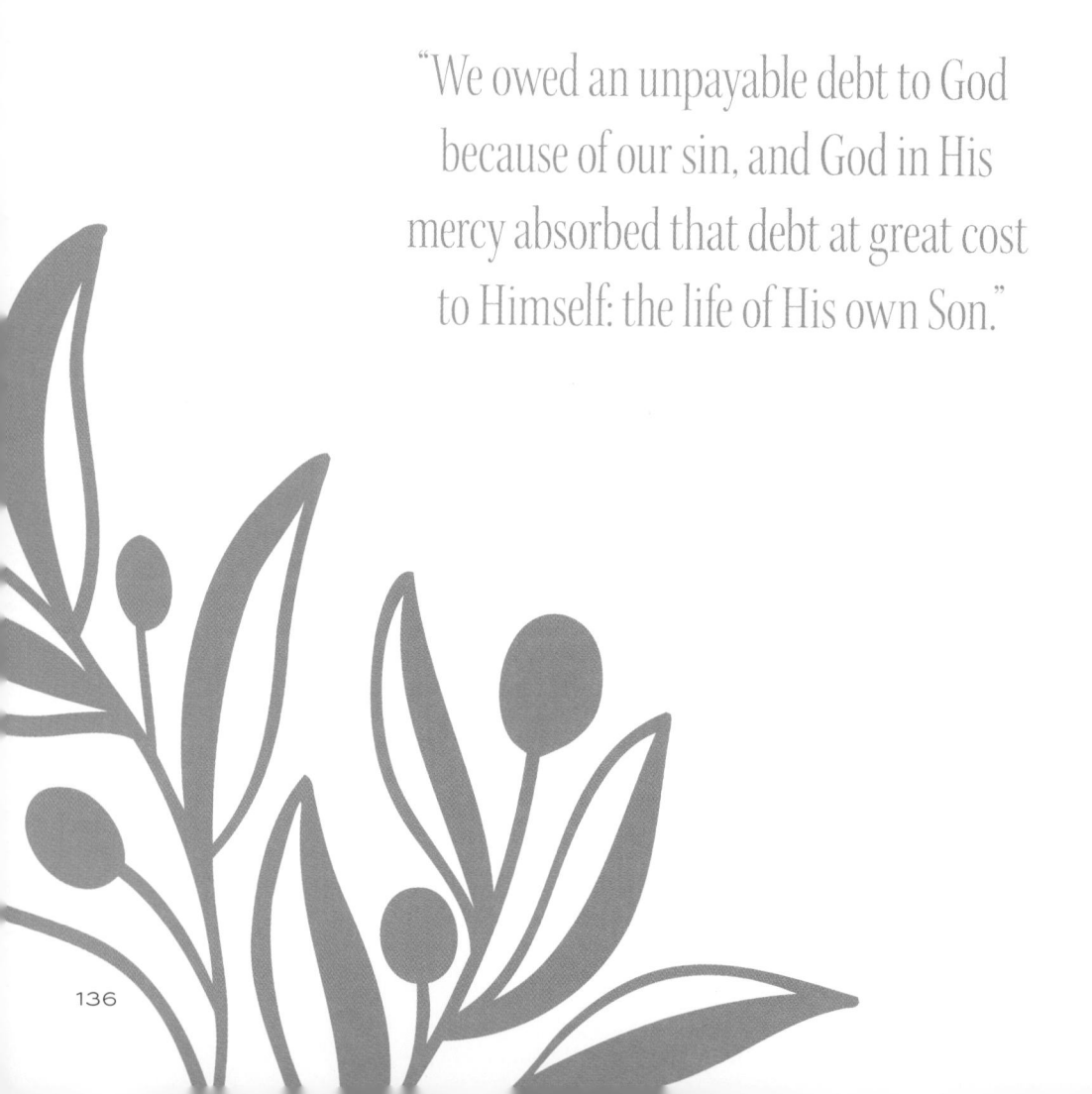

> "We owed an unpayable debt to God because of our sin, and God in His mercy absorbed that debt at great cost to Himself: the life of His own Son."

**REFLECT**

When have you found it difficult to forgive others? In what ways does Jesus's parable bring comfort to you and challenge you?

**PRAY**

Ask God to remind you of how He gave His Son, Jesus, to pay off your unpayable debt of sin. Pray that He would give you strength to extend this generosity to others in your life.

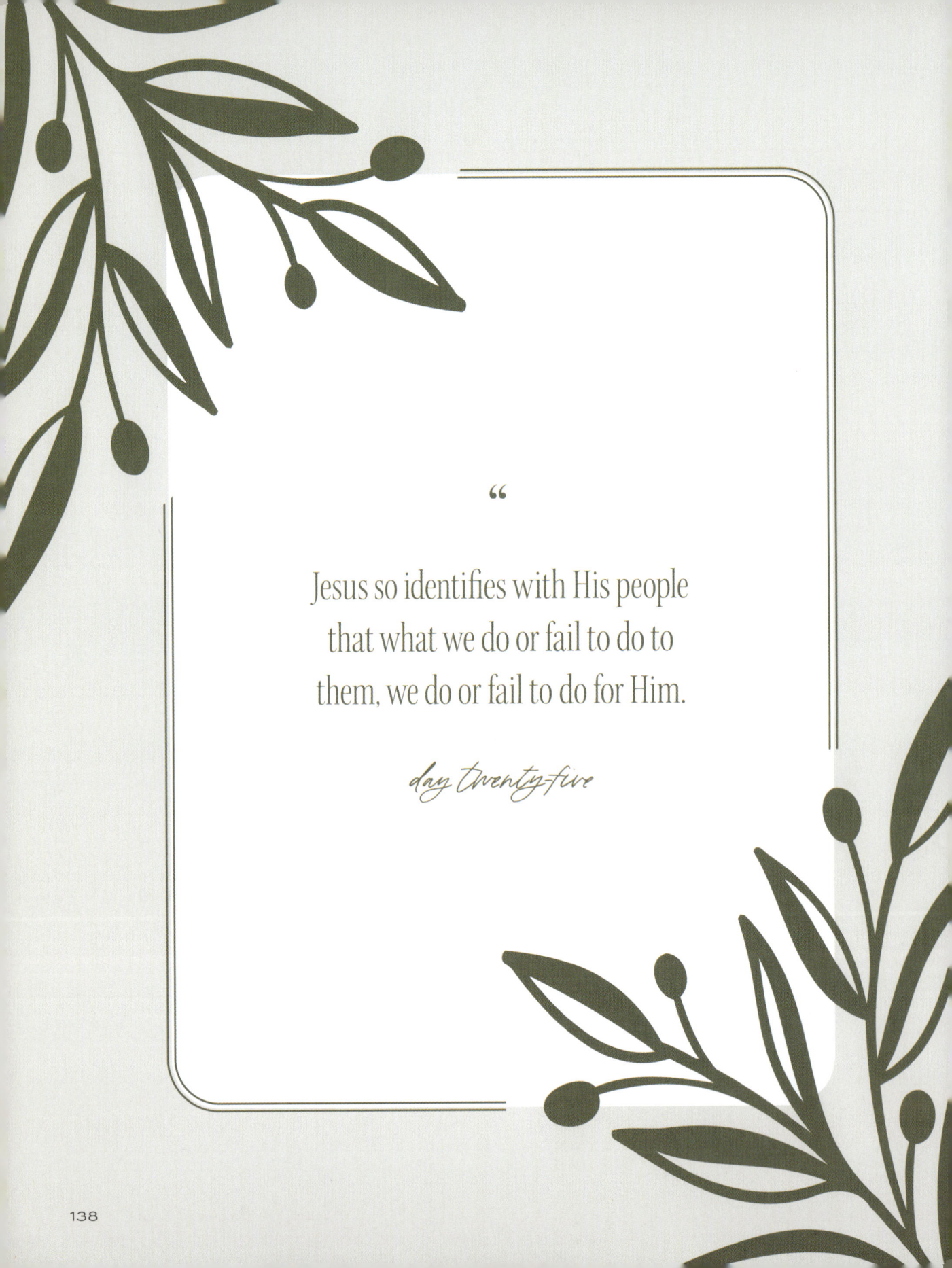

"

Jesus so identifies with His people that what we do or fail to do to them, we do or fail to do for Him.

*day twenty-five*

# The Sheep and Goats

READ MATTHEW 25:35-40

Friends do not always share the same interests. For example, your relationship with your best friend will likely not be impacted too much if you dislike their favorite movie or their favorite restaurant. But if you were to express dislike for their spouse or their children, the relationship would likely sour, because if we love someone, we will care about what is most precious to them, a point Jesus makes in Matthew 25.

Verses 31–33 set the scene: Jesus says that upon His return, He will gather the nations together for judgment. This is then illustrated by Jesus separating the sheep from the goats; the sheep on His right (the place of honor) and the goats on His left (the place of dishonor). The reason for the distinction is that the sheep, in tending to the needs of the oppressed and downtrodden, were, in reality, serving Jesus Himself (Matthew 25:34–40). But the goats, in failing to tend to their needs, were failing to serve Jesus (Matthew 25:41–46).

Scholars debate whether Jesus is speaking of serving disadvantaged Christians or disadvantaged people in general. While Jesus is clearly concerned with His followers meeting the needs of *all* types of people (as we will see in the following study day), here He seems to reference Christians specifically. This is indicated by Him calling this group His "brothers and sisters," a phrase often used in Matthew to refer to His disciples (Matthew 12:46–50, 28:10). This is also consistent with how Jesus says that to welcome one of His disciples is to welcome Him (Matthew 10:40–42). Jesus so identifies with His people that what we do or fail to do to them, we do or fail to do for Him (verses 40, 45).

To be clear, Jesus is not teaching that we are saved by works. Rather, just as children ought to imitate their Father's love for the undeserving (Luke 6:27–28) and forgiven people ought to extend that same forgiveness (Matthew 18:21–35), so too should we imitate Jesus's concern for the lowly (Matthew 11:5). If we love Jesus, we will love His representatives in this world, including the poor who, while often overlooked, are precious to Him.

It can be tempting to serve the needs of important people first, perhaps out of a desire for recognition or repayment. But that is not what Jesus did. And neither should it mark our lives who claim to be His followers. This passage challenges us to consider how we treat the poor. Our love for Jesus ought to express itself in serving the "least" — it should make us willing to be inconvenienced, for that is exactly how Jesus has loved us.

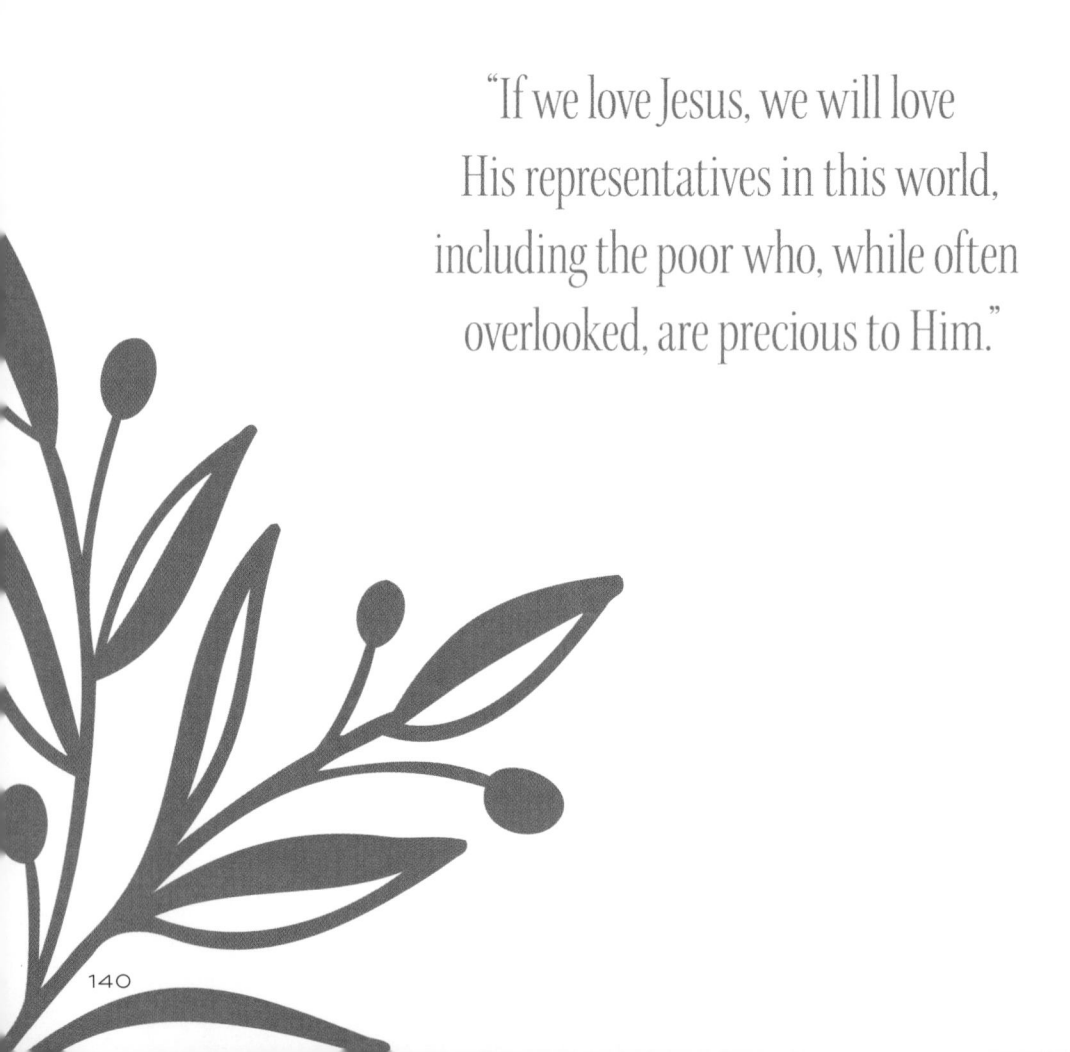

> "If we love Jesus, we will love His representatives in this world, including the poor who, while often overlooked, are precious to Him."

**REFLECT**

Is your life marked by a concern for others? How can you practically demonstrate the kind of care Jesus describes in this passage?

**PRAY**

Ask for God to help you be alert to the needs of others around you. Pray that He would help you love those who are precious to Him and remember that in serving them, you are serving Jesus.

"

Jesus teaches us that loving our neighbor involves loving all people, no matter who they are. In doing so, we reflect Christ's unconditional love for all people.

*day twenty-six*

# The Good Samaritan

READ LUKE 10:25-37

Many of us have heard the phrase "Love thy neighbor" before. While this phrase is found in Scripture, it is often spoken by people who would not consider themselves religious. After all, who would argue against loving others? But even though our world commends loving others, many people limit their love. They might say that they love others, but they actually only love those who are like them or those they are the most comfortable with. In today's passage, Jesus teaches us that loving our neighbor involves loving all people, no matter who they are. In doing so, we reflect Christ's unconditional love for all people.

In Luke 10, Jesus is questioned by a lawyer. At first, it seems as if the lawyer knows Scripture well. He understands that Scripture commands us to love God and others. Yet what the lawyer does not fully understand is who exactly he should love. This man knows that he is to love others, but is he practically living out this truth? It appears that he is not, as he seeks to justify himself by asking who his neighbor is (Luke 10:29).

While this seems like an innocent question, the motivation behind the question reveals the lawyer's lack of understanding when it comes to God's law. Jesus uses a parable to disclose this man's misunderstanding. In this parable, Jesus tells of a man, likely a Jew, who is beaten and left for dead. The crowd around Jesus would expect the first two men who pass by, a priest and a Levite, to help the beaten man because both of these men know and observe God's law. But the men do not. However, a third person comes into the scene who is completely unexpected—a Samaritan. Jews and Samaritans had a long history of feuding; therefore, the crowd would expect the Samaritan to dismiss the man. Instead, the Samaritan goes above and beyond in caring for this man.

When Jesus asks the lawyer which of the three men was a neighbor to the hurt man, the lawyer responds with the Samaritan. The lawyer acknowledges the mercy of the Samaritan, and Jesus commands the lawyer to show mercy in the same ways the Samaritan did. Through this parable, Jesus teaches that true obedience to God's law involves loving and being merciful to *all* people. Jesus has shown us what this love and mercy look like through His death and resurrection. Scripture does not tell us that Jesus loves and is merciful to *some*. Rather, Jesus loves and is merciful to *all* people, as He sacrificed Himself for all and offers salvation to all (1 John 2:2).

Jesus's parable challenges us to consider whether we are truly loving our neighbor. Are we caring for those who only look like us or loving only those who are easy to love? May the gospel challenge us to love our neighbor as ourselves, reflecting our merciful Savior as we do.

> "True obedience to God's law involves loving and being merciful to all people."

**REFLECT**

What would it look like for you to be merciful to others?

**PRAY**

Pray that you would love and care for all people and ask that God would help you when it is hard to love them.

"

As followers of Jesus, we must be humbly aware of our own faults and avoid a harsh and critical spirit toward others.

*day twenty-seven*

# Do Not Judge

READ MATTHEW 7:1–5

No one is perfect. And because of that, correction is a part of life. When a friend loses their temper with someone, we might tell them they are out of line. When a coworker messes up a task, we might inform them and show them how to perform the task properly. If we are not careful, though, we might subtly take joy in others' faults, finding that it helps us to ignore our own. But as followers of Jesus, we must be humbly aware of our own faults and avoid a harsh and critical spirit toward others.

Matthew 7:1 would likely rank among Jesus's most popular and well-known sayings, though maybe not for the right reasons. When confronted about something wrong they have done or a particular pattern of behavior, someone might turn to Matthew 7:1 as a shield to deflect criticism: *See? Jesus says not to judge, so back off!*

But when Jesus says, "Do not judge," He is not forbidding us from being discerning and making judgment calls about other people. After all, just a few verses later, when warning about false prophets, He says that we will know false prophets by how they live and act (Matthew 7:15–20). Rather, what Jesus is forbidding is a harsh and sharply critical spirit — one which makes us all too ready to point out the faults of others while remaining hypocritically oblivious to our own.

To illustrate His point, Jesus offers up a ridiculous scenario, one which likely elicited laughter from His audience. In this scenario, a person is attempting to remove a tiny splinter from another's eye while ignoring the massive beam sticking out of their own (Matthew 7:3–5). Yes, the splinter *does* need to be removed. But for someone to insist on this without doing something about the beam in their own eye is hypocritical.

This man condemns in others what he excuses in himself. And this is a warning to us who find ourselves prone to do the same. We fixate on the shortcomings of others while minimizing or excusing our own. At the heart of this hypocrisy that Jesus warns against is pride, and it causes us to be harsh toward others. But Jesus's followers are called to humility—to a greater awareness of our own sins than of the sins of others, thus uprooting self-righteousness.

Throughout this week, we have seen how our relationship with God should directly impact our relationship with others. God's children will imitate their Father's love. Those forgiven by Him will forgive others. So here we see that those to whom God has been kind ought not to be harsh and critical to others. To go searching for faults in others when God—completely aware of *our* faults—deals gently with us is inappropriate. Splinters in others need to be removed, but they should be removed in humility.

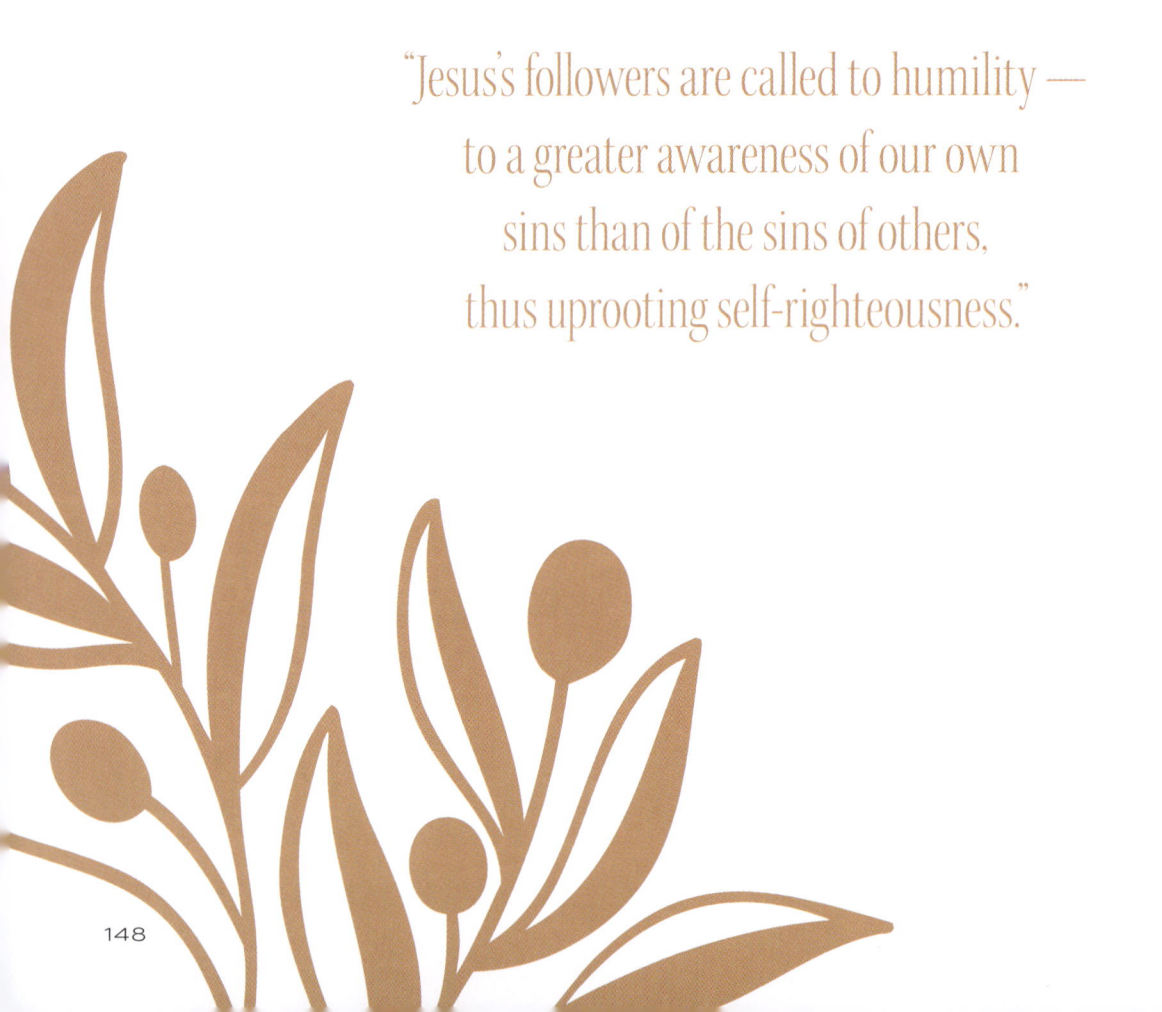

> "Jesus's followers are called to humility—
> to a greater awareness of our own
> sins than of the sins of others,
> thus uprooting self-righteousness."

**REFLECT**

Have you ever been on the receiving end of someone's hypocritical judgment? Have you ever been hypocritical yourself? How can these verses help you to be humble in your relationships?

**PRAY**

Pray first that you would regularly remember how God has been gentle and patient with you. Then pray that you might extend that same gentleness to others and flee from a harsh spirit.

"

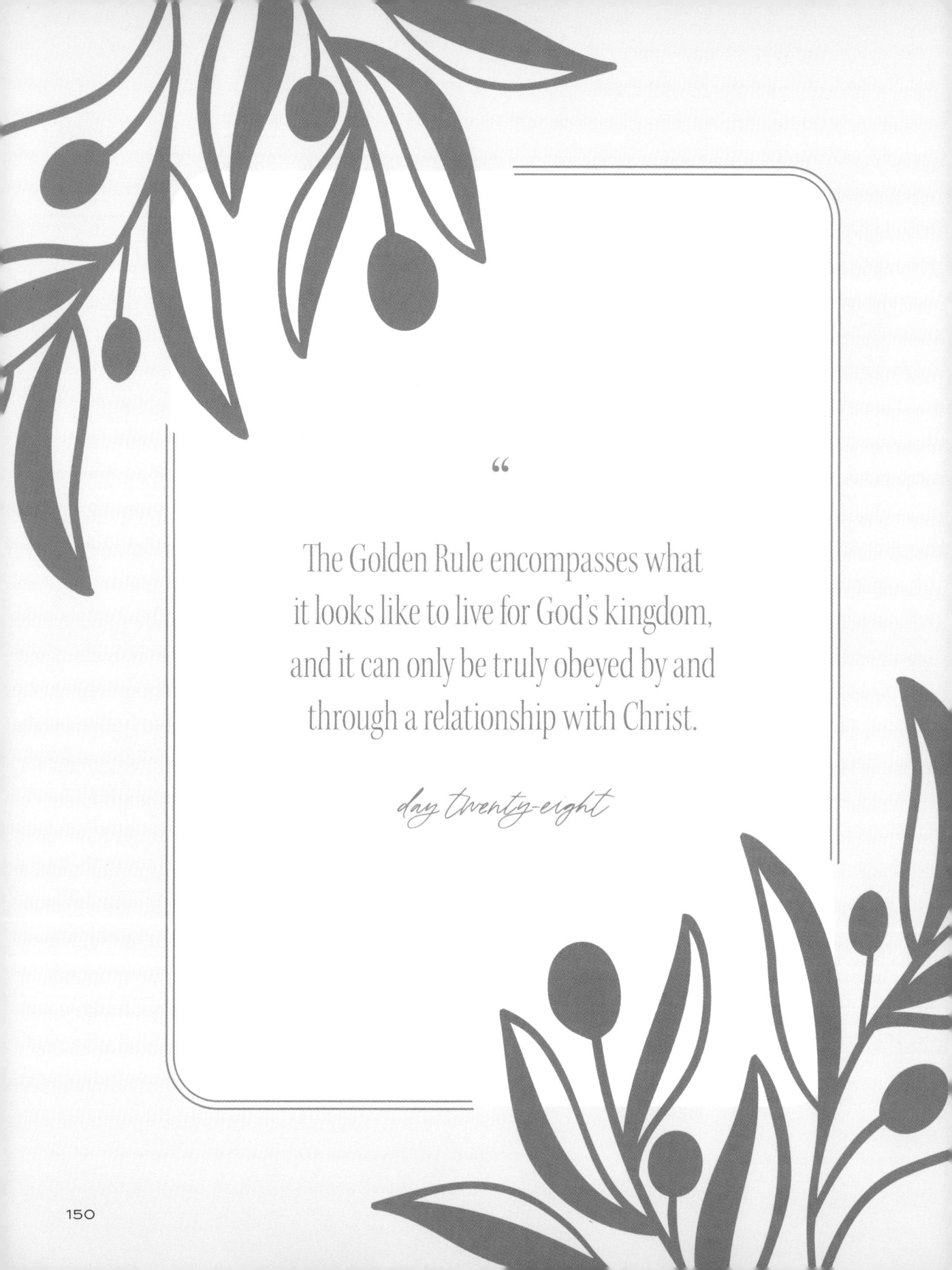

The Golden Rule encompasses what it looks like to live for God's kingdom, and it can only be truly obeyed by and through a relationship with Christ.

*day twenty-eight*

# The Golden Rule

READ MATTHEW 7:12

Many people know the Golden Rule—the command to treat others how you would want to be treated—and it is often considered a moral code to live by. This is why it is called the Golden Rule, because people ascribe high value to this command. Some know that the principle is actually found in Scripture, and even those who don't know this will often agree it is a good rule to live by, spoken by a good teacher whose way of life was admirable. But viewing this command in only this way disconnects the Golden Rule from the gospel. What Jesus teaches us in Matthew 7:12 is far from simply a good moral command to follow. The Golden Rule encompasses what it looks like to live for God's kingdom, and it can only be truly obeyed by and through a relationship with Christ.

Matthew 7:12 is part of the Sermon on the Mount, and the verse comes after Jesus's teachings that speak about asking from God and receiving from Him, trusting that God is a Father who gives good gifts to His children. The word "therefore" in verse 12 likely points back to the sum of Jesus's teachings on the kingdom of God so far. By looking back to all that has come before, we learn that living according to the Golden Rule is part of what it means to live according to God's kingdom.

Therefore, because believers belong to God's kingdom, they are the ones who are able to truly follow the Golden Rule. While those who do not follow God can treat others with kindness, only through a relationship with Christ is one able to reflect Christ's kindness and love. When reciting the Golden Rule, people tend to leave out the latter portion: "for this is the Law and the Prophets." These words mean that the Golden Rule summarizes what the Old Testament is all about: loving God and loving others.

Galatians 5:14 says something similar: "For the whole law is fulfilled in one statement: Love your neighbor as yourself." The only way we can truly love God and others is through a relationship with Christ.

Only One has followed the Golden Rule perfectly, and that is Jesus Christ. Jesus gave freely, expecting nothing in return. And He treated all people with the same level of respect and love. Jesus fully obeyed this command, and therefore the Law as a whole, as He perfectly loved God and others. While Jesus is the only One who fully obeyed the Golden Rule, it is through our relationship with Christ and by the Holy Spirit that we are able to follow this command. As we daily rely on the Holy Spirit, we will treat others the way we want to be treated, reflecting Christ's love in the process.

> "The only way we can truly love God and others is through a relationship with Christ."

**REFLECT**

How are you currently treating others? How can you treat those around you the way you would like to be treated?

**PRAY**

Thank Jesus for enabling you to treat others rightly because of His power within you. Pray that you will seek to treat others the way you want to be treated.

*week 5 conclusion*

Jesus calls us to a high standard in our relationships with others. We are to actively seek out the good of those who hate us, to forgive those who have hurt us, to care for the vulnerable we are tempted to ignore, and to treat them exactly how we would want to be treated. But as we have seen, God has done far more for us than He calls us to do for others. For example, though forgiving others can be extraordinarily difficult, we must remember that God has forgiven much more in us. Before moving on to the next week, ask God to reveal to you ways that you can practically extend His love to others.

> God has done far more for us than
> He calls us to do for others.

*week 6*

# Jesus's Words on the Cost of Following Him

## memory verse

Calling the crowd along with his disciples, he said to them, "If anyone wants to follow after me, let him deny himself, take up his cross, and follow me."

MARK 8:34

## introduction

In the first week, we saw that one of the reasons Jesus came was to call followers to Himself. And ever since, we have explored many aspects of Jesus that make Him worth following. He is the Bread of Life who satisfies our souls. He promises us rest, teaches us about God's love for us, and calls us to love others. Our hearts rightly long to follow someone like this! But following Him comes with a cost, because His path is a path that involves suffering. But it does not *end* in suffering. As we will see this week, following Jesus is costly, but it is most certainly worth it.

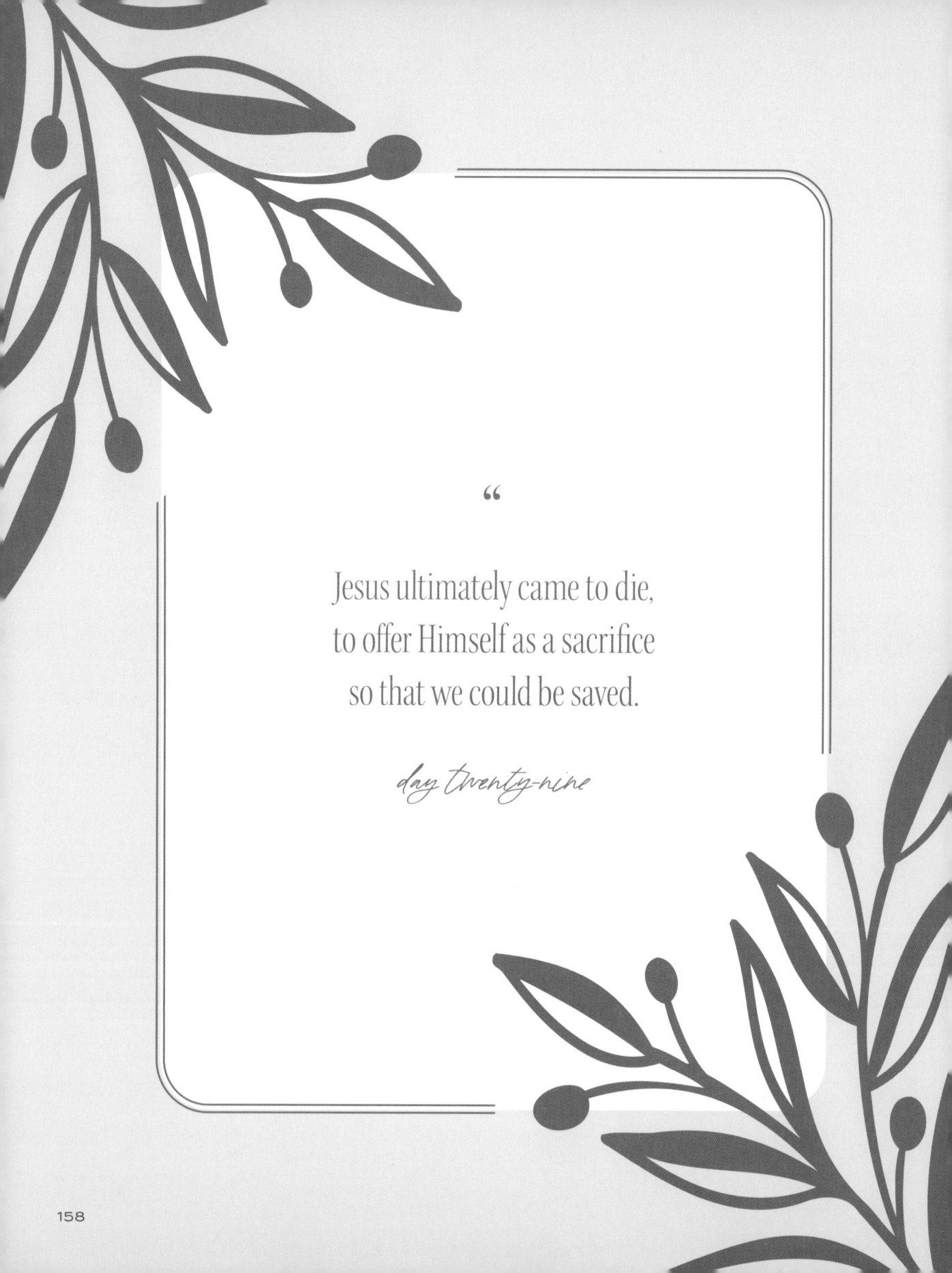

> Jesus ultimately came to die,
> to offer Himself as a sacrifice
> so that we could be saved.
>
> *day twenty-nine*

# Jesus Must Suffer

READ LUKE 9:21–22

Jesus's ministry is something to marvel about. Over the course of His ministry, Jesus opened the eyes of the blind, cured diseases, and even raised dead people to life. He taught many sermons and spoke many parables that proclaimed the truth of God's kingdom and invited others to be a part of God's kingdom. But Jesus's time on earth did not involve only miracles and teachings. Jesus ultimately came to die, to offer Himself as a sacrifice so that we could be saved. Jesus did not disclose this information to His disciples in the beginning of His ministry, but over time, He revealed to them what was to come. In the passage we read today, Jesus predicts His coming death and resurrection to His disciples, revealing how His death is necessary in order to bring about salvation.

Luke 9:21–22 takes place after Peter makes an important confession. When Jesus asks His disciples who people say He is, His disciples respond by saying John the Baptist, the prophet Elijah, or another ancient prophet (Luke 9:19). But then, Jesus shifts His question by asking His disciples, "who do you say that I am?" Peter responds by saying that Jesus is "God's Messiah" (Luke 9:20). In doing so, Peter confesses and declares that Jesus is the promised Messiah, the One God said would come to establish salvation and restoration (Isaiah 42:1–4).

Jesus tells His disciples not to tell anyone about this truth (Luke 9:21). He follows up this warning by making the first of three predictions about His death and resurrection, making it clear what will happen. He will suffer, be rejected, be killed, and will be raised on the third day. Luke does not record any reaction or response from the disciples but instead seems to focus on what will happen to Jesus, specifically His suffering.

The Jews and the disciples expected the Messiah to come with power and victory, overthrowing Rome and providing peace for the Jews as a result. But Jesus would accomplish victory in a different way, by sacrificing Himself on the cross. There on the cross, Jesus would take on the weight of our sin, allowing Himself to be punished for our sake. But this would not be the end, for three days later, He would rise from the dead, declaring His victory over the power of sin and death.

This is why Jesus says in verse 22 that "it is necessary" for the Son of Man, or Himself, to die. It was necessary for Jesus to suffer, die, and be raised from the dead because in doing so, He accomplished salvation for all who trust and believe in Him. While it would take time for Jesus's disciples to understand this truth, today we have the opportunity to receive and respond to this truth by accepting the salvation Jesus gave up His life to make possible. Because Jesus's death and resurrection were necessary, we can be saved and declared forgiven.

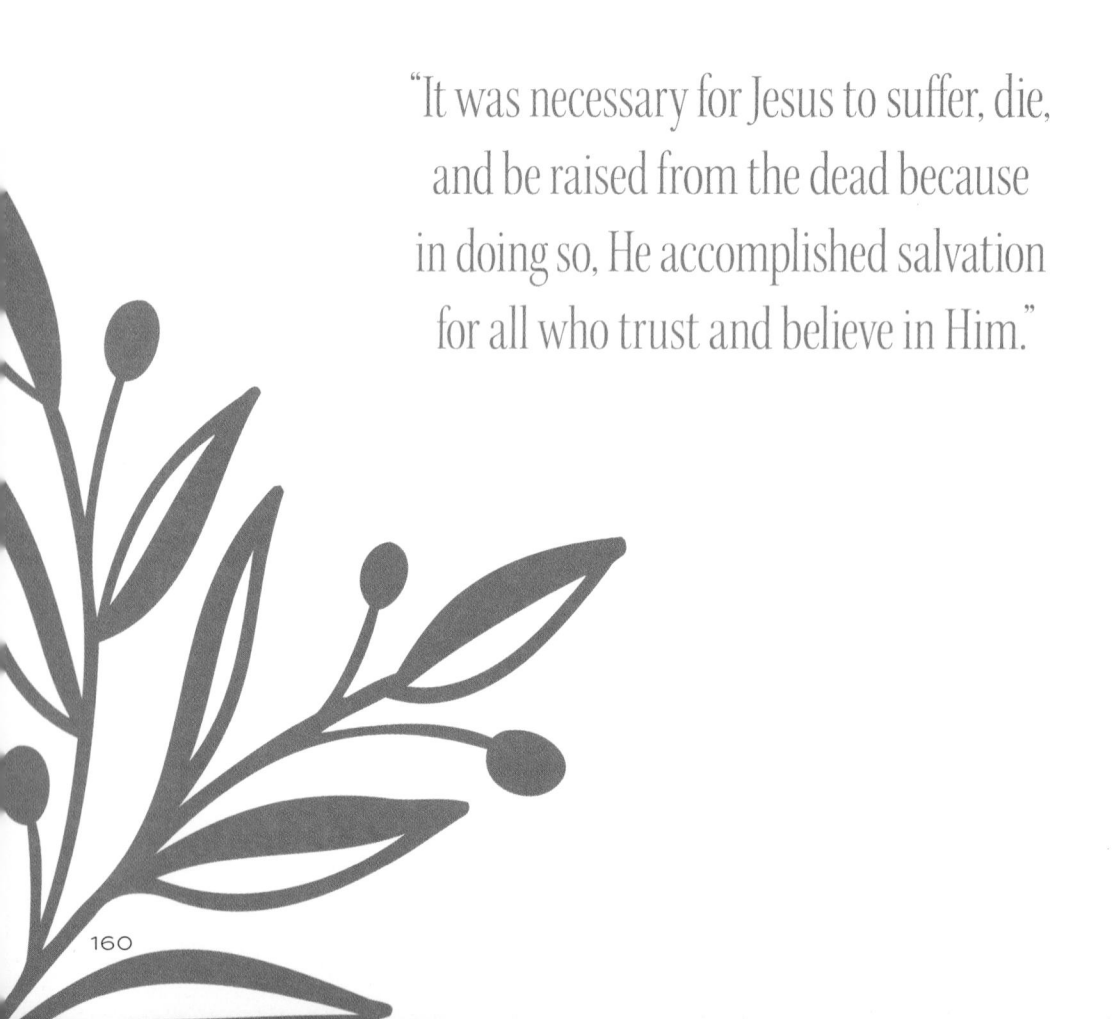

> "It was necessary for Jesus to suffer, die, and be raised from the dead because in doing so, He accomplished salvation for all who trust and believe in Him."

**REFLECT**

How does it humble you to know that Jesus willingly chose to die for you?

**PRAY**

Thank Jesus for choosing to die on the cross so that you could be saved. Pray that you would live daily in light of His sacrifice for you through your worship and obedience to Him.

> "As Jesus's disciples, we must relinquish self-interest and self-determination.

*day thirty*

# Deny Yourself, Take Up Your Cross, and Follow Me

READ MARK 8:34-35

"Follow the leader" is a children's game with a fun and simple premise: a child is appointed as the leader, and the other children have to go where that child goes and do what they do. The game serves as a fitting metaphor for the Christian life, in which Jesus is the leader and we are His followers. But as Jesus makes crystal clear to His would-be followers, following Him comes with an enormous cost.

Back on Day 4, we saw that part of what Jesus came to do was to gather followers who would carry on His work in the world after His ascension to heaven. "Follow me," He said to Simon, Andrew, James, and John, who dropped what they were doing and reoriented their lives around Him (Mark 1:16–20). While such reorientation was already costly, the revelation that Jesus must suffer and die introduced a cost they were not prepared for. Not only would Jesus die, but so too could those who follow Him expect to suffer.

Gathering to Himself a crowd alongside His disciples, Jesus clearly tells them that anyone who wants to be His disciple must deny themselves, take up their cross, and follow Him (Mark 8:34). This makes sense. After all, if Jesus—the leader—will suffer and die, then those who follow the leader can expect the same. Still, it ought to force us to consider whether being a disciple of Jesus is worth it as it involves doing things that do not come naturally to us.

First, being a disciple involves denying ourselves. As Jesus's disciples, we must relinquish self-interest and self-determination. We must be willing to sacrifice whatever agendas we have—personal, professional, financial, etc.—if pursuing them conflicts with pursuing Jesus.

Second, it involves taking up our cross. Crucifixion was a brutal form of execution that combined physical and emotional anguish. Those condemned to such a fate would have to carry their cross to the place of their crucifixion—a shameful march, which would likely be accompanied by jeers from onlookers. Disciples must be willing to face death and the scorn of this world.

Finally, discipleship involves following Jesus. Disciples must possess a determination to keep going—to continue following Jesus no matter how inconvenient the path is or how much rejection from others we receive.

Despite this heavy cost, though, we continue to follow the leader because we see that His path did not end with death. Jesus rose from the dead and is currently exalted at God's right hand. Following Him will, therefore, lead us through suffering now in this life, but the path will come out on the other side of death, where we will share in His glory. And so Jesus reminds His audience that "whoever loses his life because of me and the gospel will save it" (Mark 8:35). What comfort and hope we have in this truth!

> "Disciples must possess a determination to keep going — to continue following Jesus no matter how inconvenient the path is or how much rejection from others we receive."

**REFLECT**

How have you experienced the cost of being a disciple of Jesus? Are there any personal agendas that are keeping you from putting Him first in your life?

**PRAY**

Ask that God would help you stay focused on following Jesus. Pray also that you would be constantly reminded of the glorious future that awaits you as a disciple.

"

Disciples of Christ are to reflect
Jesus by choosing to serve
rather than be served.

*day thirty-one*

# Serve Instead of Being Served

READ MARK 10:42–45

Desiring glory is part of our sinful nature. Even those of us who consider ourselves humble know what it is like to feel that rush of pride when we are praised or that twinge of jealousy when someone receives praise instead of us. Being in a high position where people look to us and praise us feels good. While it is not necessarily wrong to be in a high position or receive praise, it is wrong to become prideful because of our position or to use our position to hurt others. In Mark 10:42–45, we learn of the disciples' own struggle with pride, and in the process, we learn that disciples of Christ are to reflect Jesus by choosing to serve rather than be served.

Mark 10:42–45 takes place after James and John ask Jesus to sit at His right hand in glory. Being at Jesus's right hand in heaven is the highest position; therefore, both James and John want to be in this place of honor. When the other disciples hear that James and John made this request, they are angry at them. However, their anger is likely due to the fact that they want this position as well. Clearly, the disciples are struggling with pride and what it looks like to truly be a disciple of Christ. So Jesus takes this moment to teach His disciples a valuable lesson on humility.

Jesus instructs that his disciples are to be different from those in leadership by choosing to serve rather than be served. He does not want His disciples to lord over others and act as tyrants because of a position of power. Instead, He desires for His disciples to care more about others than themselves, choosing to serve others humbly. If the disciples need a reason to serve others in this way, Jesus reminds them how He has come to earth not to be served but to serve.

The disciples are struggling with pride because they believe that their position as disciples of Jesus, the Messiah, gives them power, or elevates them above others. What the disciples fail to recognize, however, is that Jesus has not come to flaunt His power as King but to serve others humbly. While Jesus will eventually return in power to fulfill God's promises to bring about restoration (Philippians 2:9–11), He came first as a humble sin offering (Philippians 2:8). Jesus's words to His disciples demonstrate that God's kingdom is more about sacrifice and service than power and prestige. When His disciples accept this reality, they will reflect Jesus by choosing to give and serve.

For those of us in Christ, we too are called to reflect Jesus in this way. Rather than seeking power and glory, we are to humbly serve others. And in the moments we struggle to do so, we can remind ourselves of Jesus's sacrifice and allow His incredible act of service to encourage our own service to others.

> "God's kingdom is more about sacrifice and service than power and prestige."

**REFLECT**

How do you struggle to serve rather than be served?
How can Jesus's sacrifice for you encourage you to serve others?

**PRAY**

Pray that the gospel would encourage you to serve others and that you would reflect Christ through your service to others. Ask God to help you in the moments you desire power and glory—that you would choose to humble yourself instead when those moments arise.

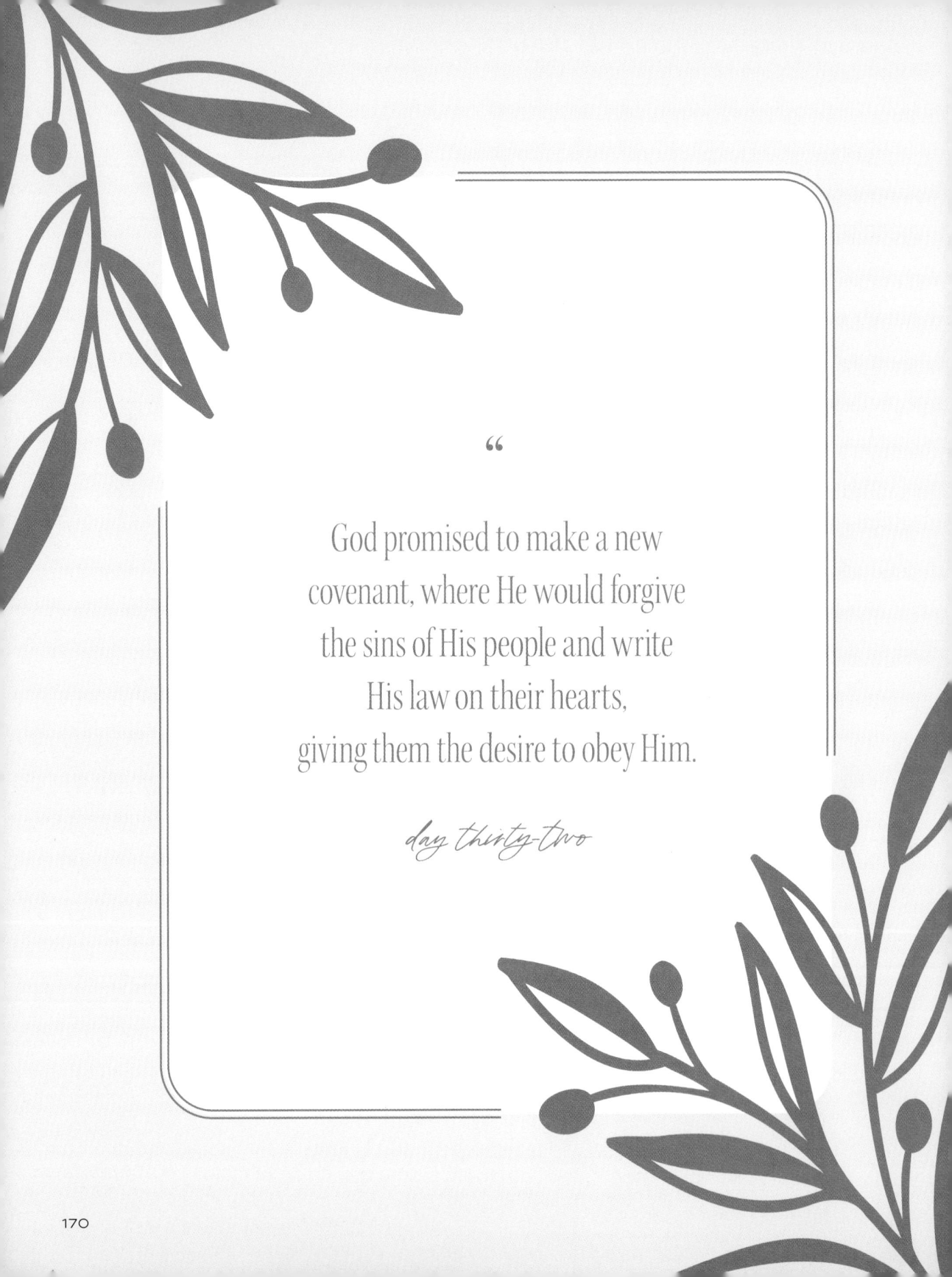

> God promised to make a new covenant, where He would forgive the sins of His people and write His law on their hearts, giving them the desire to obey Him.

*day thirty-two*

# This Is My Body and Blood

READ LUKE 22:19-20

In any given year, we likely commemorate many important occasions in some way: anniversaries, birthdays, holidays, and certain dates that may hold personal significance for us. In commemorating these reasons for celebration, we pause to reflect on the past and how the given date is significant to our lives in the present. Likewise, at Jesus's final meal before His crucifixion—what we call the Lord's Supper—He instructed His disciples to continually commemorate His death in order to dwell on the significance of the cross and Christ's sacrifice for our deliverance.

To appreciate the Lord's Supper, it is important to recall Israel's deliverance from Egypt. After nine plagues in which God demonstrated His superiority over Pharaoh and Egypt's gods, God sent a tenth and final plague that would claim the lives of all the firstborn sons in Egypt. Israel would be spared this fate if they killed a lamb and painted the doorposts of their homes with its blood. Upon seeing this blood, God would then pass over their homes. This event, which led Pharaoh to release the Israelites, became known as Passover, and it was to be commemorated annually with a meal. The Passover meal recalled how God saved His people from slavery and then entered into a covenant relationship with them at Mount Sinai.

It is this meal that Jesus and His disciples are eating on the night before His crucifixion (Luke 22:7–8). Interestingly, though, Jesus re-centers the meaning of this meal around Himself. After breaking the bread and handing it to His disciples, Jesus says, "This is my body, which is given for you" (Luke 22:19). Jesus's body will be broken "for" them. And they should eat the bread in "remembrance"—or commemoration—of Him.

Similarly, Jesus takes the cup of wine and calls it "the new covenant in my blood, which is poured out for you" (Luke 22:20). Again, Jesus is referencing His death, and a particularly violent one at that. And again, He states that it will be "for" them. But what will His death do for them exactly?

The answer is found in the "new covenant" language, which is taken from Jeremiah 31:31–34. After God rescued Israel from Egypt and entered into a covenant with them, Israel ended up breaking that covenant through their sinful ways. But through Jeremiah, God promised to make a new covenant, where He would forgive the sins of His people and write His law on their hearts, giving them the desire to obey Him. *That*, Jesus is saying, *is what my death will accomplish.*

And that is what we commemorate today whenever we take the Lord's Supper. As we partake of the bread and the wine, we recall our own deliverance—not from slavery in Egypt but slavery to sin and death. We celebrate the forgiveness of sins and the promise of eternal life that is ours because Jesus took on Himself the punishment our sins deserved. We celebrate that because Jesus died for us, God has passed over our sins and made us His children.

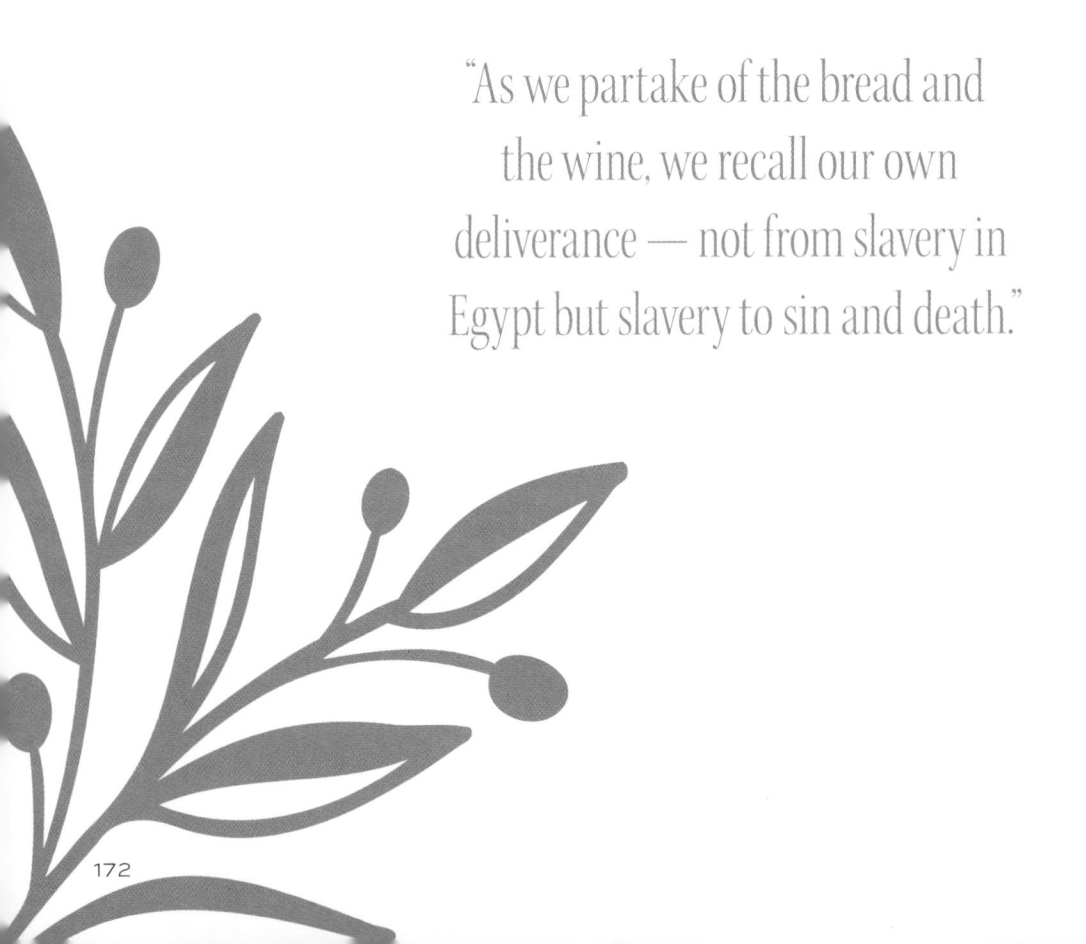

> "As we partake of the bread and the wine, we recall our own deliverance — not from slavery in Egypt but slavery to sin and death."

**REFLECT**

Why is it so important to commemorate what Jesus has done for us? How does the Passover help us to appreciate the Lord's Supper?

**PRAY**

Spend time thanking God for delivering you from slavery to sin and death and for bringing you into a relationship with Himself through Jesus.

"
When faced with intense pressure,
Jesus perfectly obeyed His Father.

*day thirty-three*

# Take This Cup Away from Me

READ MARK 14:36

*Folding under pressure.*

*Cracking under pressure.*

*The straw that broke the camel's back.*

Phrases like these are used to communicate that while all of us can withstand some degree of pressure, eventually there comes a point when it becomes too much for us to bear. While these phrases could probably describe moments from all of our lives, they cannot be said to describe Jesus, for when faced with intense pressure, Jesus perfectly obeyed His Father.

In Mark 14:32–42, we find Jesus with His disciples in the garden of Gethsemane, a scene which occurs right before His arrest and one in which we are clearly reminded of Jesus's humanity as He feels the weight of what is coming. Though Jesus has been speaking to His disciples about His impending death, we now see His emotional response to it. After telling His disciples that He is "deeply grieved to the point of death" (Mark 14:34)—words which echo the psalmist's feelings of anguish in Psalm 42:5–6, 11—Jesus goes off to pray.

Mark gives His own summary of what Jesus prays for in verse 35—that "the hour might pass from him." In verse 36, we read Jesus's actual words: "Take this cup away from me." In many places in Scripture, the "cup" is a metaphor for God's judgment (Psalm 75:8, Isaiah 51:17, Ezekiel 23:32–34), and Jesus had already referred to His death in this way earlier in Mark's Gospel (Mark 10:38).

The cup metaphor helps us to understand Jesus's agony here. He is not merely agonizing over the physical suffering that is to come His way in the form of flogging and crucifixion (though that may certainly be part of it). He is agonizing over bearing in

Himself the wrath and judgment of God. A terrible ordeal awaits Him—something far worse than the extreme physical pain to come—and one that He prays "might pass from him" if possible (verse 35).

With His emotions and agony on full display, we are reminded in this scene that Jesus is not only truly God but truly human. He understands our weaknesses and was "tempted in every way as we are" (Hebrews 4:15). This moment "assures us that he understands our darkest hours" (Ferguson, 239).

Yet in the midst of this darkness, Jesus demonstrates remarkable resiliency. He refers to God as "*Abba*," or "Father," a word that expresses Jesus's intimacy with and trust in God. And He prays, "Nevertheless, not what I will, but what you will" (verse 36). Even Jesus's reference to Psalm 42 is an expression of trust, since it is a psalm in which the author, though in despair, resolves to trust in God, knowing that God will vindicate him. In His darkest moments, Jesus entrusted Himself to His Father, and because He persevered, we can now have eternal life.

> "With His emotions and agony on full display, we are reminded in this scene that Jesus is not only truly God but truly human."

**REFLECT**

In what ways has obedience to God's will been costly for you? What encouragement can you take from this scene in Mark 14?

**PRAY**

Spend time meditating on Jesus's costly endurance and praise Him for His perseverance. Pray that God would help you to persevere when following Him is difficult.

> Jesus says that those who currently sit in judgment over Him will one day sit under His judgment.

*day thirty-four*

# You Will See the Son of Man

READ MATTHEW 26:64

In his letter to the church of Philippi, the Apostle Paul beautifully recounts the life of Jesus as one full of contrasts. Though Jesus, as God, has eternally existed, He nevertheless emptied Himself and took on the form of a servant (Philippians 2:6–7). And after humbling Himself to the point of being crucified, Jesus was highly exalted (Philippians 2:8–11). These contrasts are on full display in Matthew 26, where Jesus says that those who currently sit in judgment over Him will one day sit under His judgment.

At this point in Jesus's life, He has already spoken several times about His impending arrest and execution. These events are now in full swing. Having been arrested in the garden of Gethsemane, Jesus now finds Himself on trial before the Sanhedrin, the Jewish ruling council, which was presided over by the high priest.

But justice is not the goal of this trial. The Sanhedrin already knows the outcome they want: Jesus's death. They just need to find some justification for it. That they bring witnesses forward shows that they want to at least *appear* as though they are following the Old Testament laws regarding such proceedings (Deuteronomy 17:6, 19:15). But the witnesses' statements do not agree (Matthew 26:60, Mark 14:56, 59). The Sanhedrin is getting nowhere.

So Caiaphas, the high priest, takes a different approach. Putting Jesus—who has been silent—under oath, he implores Him directly: "Tell us if you are the Messiah, the Son of God" (Matthew 26:63). It is a political maneuver on Caiaphas's part. Only the Romans had the authority at this time to carry out capital punishment, so if Jesus declares Himself to be the "Messiah"—a king—the Sanhedrin can then paint Him as a rival to Caesar and let the Romans take care of Him.

Jesus replies in the affirmative, but adds that "in the future you will see the Son of Man seated at the right hand of Power and coming on the clouds of heaven" (Matthew 26:64). It is this explosive comment that finally gives Caiaphas a reason for having Jesus killed. By referring to Himself as the figure described in Daniel 7:13–14 and Psalm 110:1 who would sit at God's right hand and be given authority to rule, Jesus is claiming divine honor for Himself and that He will sit in judgment over God's enemies, including them. Therefore, Jesus is not the one on trial here — they are.

This is followed by Caiaphas's charge of blasphemy and the Sanhedrin members beating, mocking, and spitting on Jesus (Matthew 26:65–67). This is part of the humiliation Paul describes in Philippians 2:5–11. But it will soon give way to the exaltation Paul describes in that same passage. Though Matthew 26 shows Jesus on trial, He now sits enthroned in heaven. And a day will come when "every knee will bow . . . and every tongue will confess that Jesus Christ is Lord" (Philippians 2:10–11).

> "Jesus is claiming divine honor for Himself and that He will sit in judgment over God's enemies."

**REFLECT**

How does seeing Jesus's sufferings in this passage help us to appreciate His love for us?

**PRAY**

Pray that God would fill your heart with love for Jesus, who suffered for us that we might be saved. Ask Him to strengthen you that you might follow the path He walked—a path of suffering now but glory later.

## week 6 conclusion

Jesus's path is a path that leads through suffering, and so it is the same path that those who would follow Jesus can expect to walk. Jesus made it clear that following Him involves an enormous cost. But any sacrifices we make to follow Jesus are worth it because while Jesus's path leads *through* suffering, it *ends* in glory—both for Him and for us. Though He hung on a cross, He now sits enthroned at the right hand of the Father in heaven, and from there He will return to establish His kingdom in its fullness. Pray that God would help you to live your life with an eye toward this future and that this future would help you to endure the sufferings now that come with following Jesus.

> Though He hung on a cross, He now sits enthroned at the right hand of the Father in heaven, and from there He will return to establish His kingdom in its fullness.

*week 7*

# Jesus's Words from the Cross

## memory verse

Then Jesus said, "Father, forgive them, because they do not know what they are doing." And they divided his clothes and cast lots.

**LUKE 23:34**

## introduction

Christians have long spoken of Jesus's "Seven Sayings" or "Seven Words" from the cross. These are seven distinct statements, compiled from the four Gospels, that were made by Jesus while He was hanging on the cross. This week, we will look at each of these sayings, with the fifth and sixth sayings being covered together on Day 39. As we consider these sayings, we will see much about Jesus's heart for sinners, His devotion to the Father, and ultimately, His victory.

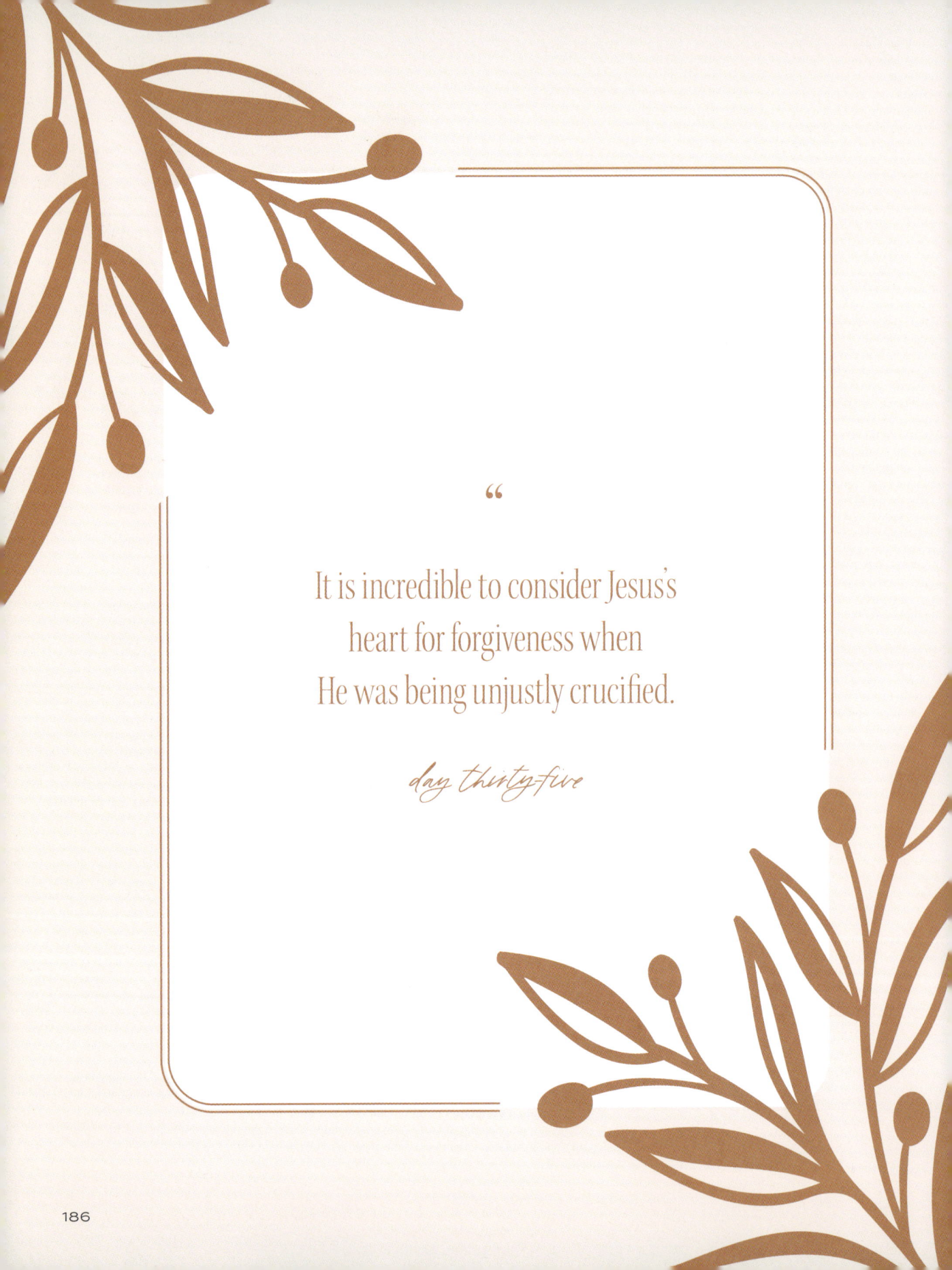

"

It is incredible to consider Jesus's heart for forgiveness when He was being unjustly crucified.

*day thirty-five*

# Father, Forgive Them

READ LUKE 23:32–34

What is your response when someone hurts you? Our first reaction is often to become angry, say something mean, or hurt them in the same way to get back at them. We usually do not feel a desire to be kind and forgive. When Jesus hung on the cross, we might believe it would have been justifiable for Jesus to retaliate in some sort of way. After all, He was being unjustly killed. But in Luke 23:34, we see Jesus respond entirely differently, teaching us that we are to forgive, even when forgiveness is undeserved.

Before Jesus went to the cross, He was severely ridiculed and mocked. He was surrounded by people who accused Him of crimes He did not commit. He was dressed in king's colors, teased as being king of the Jews, even though in reality He is indeed the true King (Luke 23:11, Matthew 27:27–31). And when Jesus stood before Pilate, the people did not relent in their cruelty. They shouted for Jesus to be crucified, allowing a guilty man to go free so that Jesus, innocent though He was, could be put to death (Luke 23:18–23).

So Jesus was crucified and hung between two criminals. As Jesus hung on the cross and looked down on those who put Him there, He did not shout in anger. He did not return their mockery. He did not curse them or tell them all the ways they were wrong. Jesus could have even asked God to send immediate punishment upon those who mocked and crucified Him. But Jesus did not do any of these things. Instead, He prayed that God would forgive them.

It is incredible to consider Jesus's heart for forgiveness when He was being unjustly crucified. He understood that those who crucified Him did so because they were lost in their sin. Their sin blinded them to the truth that Jesus was the Son of God, and they were crucifying Him despite His innocence. Even though these people deserved to be punished, Jesus had compassion on them and asked that they would be forgiven. Jesus's prayer was answered by His own sacrifice, as through His death and resurrection, all those who place their trust in Him are forgiven.

Although we were not the ones who physically put Jesus on the cross, we are all guilty for our sin. Apart from Christ, we are blind to our sin, ignorant to how pursuing sin only leads us further away from God and toward death. But because of Christ's mercy and His work on the cross, we are able to be forgiven, undeserving as we are. We are able to have our sins washed away and our guilt cleared. If we are in Christ, we are called to reflect our forgiving Savior. Though it might be hard to extend compassion and mercy when someone hurts us, when we consider the gospel, we are humbled and encouraged to forgive. Because Christ forgave us, we can forgive others.

> "Because of Christ's mercy and His work on the cross, we are able to be forgiven, undeserving as we are."

**REFLECT**

How does Christ's forgiveness on the cross encourage your own forgiveness to others?

**PRAY**

Pray that you will reflect Christ's forgiveness by forgiving others, asking for God's help to do so when forgiveness feels hard.

> When we humbly acknowledge
> our sins and cling to Jesus
> in faith, we will be saved.

*day thirty-six*

# Today You Will Be with Me in Paradise

READ LUKE 23:43

On Day 1, we looked at Jesus's first words in Mark's Gospel, which summarize His message: "Repent and believe" (Mark 1:15). Now, at the end of Jesus's life, we see an unexpected person heed this summons. And through his interaction with Jesus, we are reminded that when we humbly acknowledge our sins and cling to Jesus in faith, we will be saved.

Hanging on the cross, Jesus is surrounded by mocking voices. There are the scoffs from the leaders, who say, "He saved others; let him save himself if this is God's Messiah, the Chosen One" (Luke 23:35). There are the Romans soldiers who offer Him sour wine and mockingly refer to Him as "the king of the Jews" (verse 36). And then there are the taunts of one of the crucified criminals: "Aren't you the Messiah? Save yourself and us!" (verse 39).

Mockery to these people probably seemed justified. The soldiers' words are likely a reminder of who the "true" king is: Caesar. It is their way of saying, *Look where this man's delusion got Him. Look what happens when you rebel against Rome.* And for many of the Jews present, the Messiah was expected to be a military conqueror, one who would rise up and *defeat* the Romans, not be humiliated by them. But by drawing our attention to the inscription hanging above Jesus's head, Luke reminds us that it is *because* Jesus is King that He is on the cross.

And a King is precisely who the other crucified criminal sees when he sees Jesus.

This unnamed man first issues a rebuke to his fellow criminal. They are there, he says, because they deserve to be. But not Jesus. He is innocent. Then the criminal makes a request of this King: "Jesus, remember me when you come into your kingdom." It is a cry for salvation, a plea to be included in the kingdom he knows Jesus will reign over. It is a remarkable display of faith and one that Jesus responds to by giving this man more than he requested. Not only will he have a place in Jesus's kingdom *one day*, but *today*: "Truly I tell you, today you will be with me in paradise" (Luke 23:43).

This scene provides a vivid demonstration of what salvation entails. There is the sinner who, by faith, sees Jesus for who He really is and clings to Him for salvation. And there is Jesus Himself who, by refusing to save Himself as requested by the mocking crowds, provides salvation to those who come to Him in faith. Because He did not save Himself, we who respond to Him in faith are assured a place in His kingdom. And we are assured, as Paul was, that when we depart this life, we will "be with Christ" (Philippians 1:23).

> "The criminal makes a request of this King: 'Jesus, remember me when you come into your kingdom.'"

**REFLECT**

Read Ephesians 2:8–9. How does the repentant thief demonstrate the truth that we are "saved by grace through faith" and "not from works"? What encouragement can you take from this?

**PRAY**

Pray that God would daily remind you that your salvation is due to God's grace and is not a reward for your good works. Repent of any ways that you are tempted to base your acceptance with God on what you do or avoid doing.

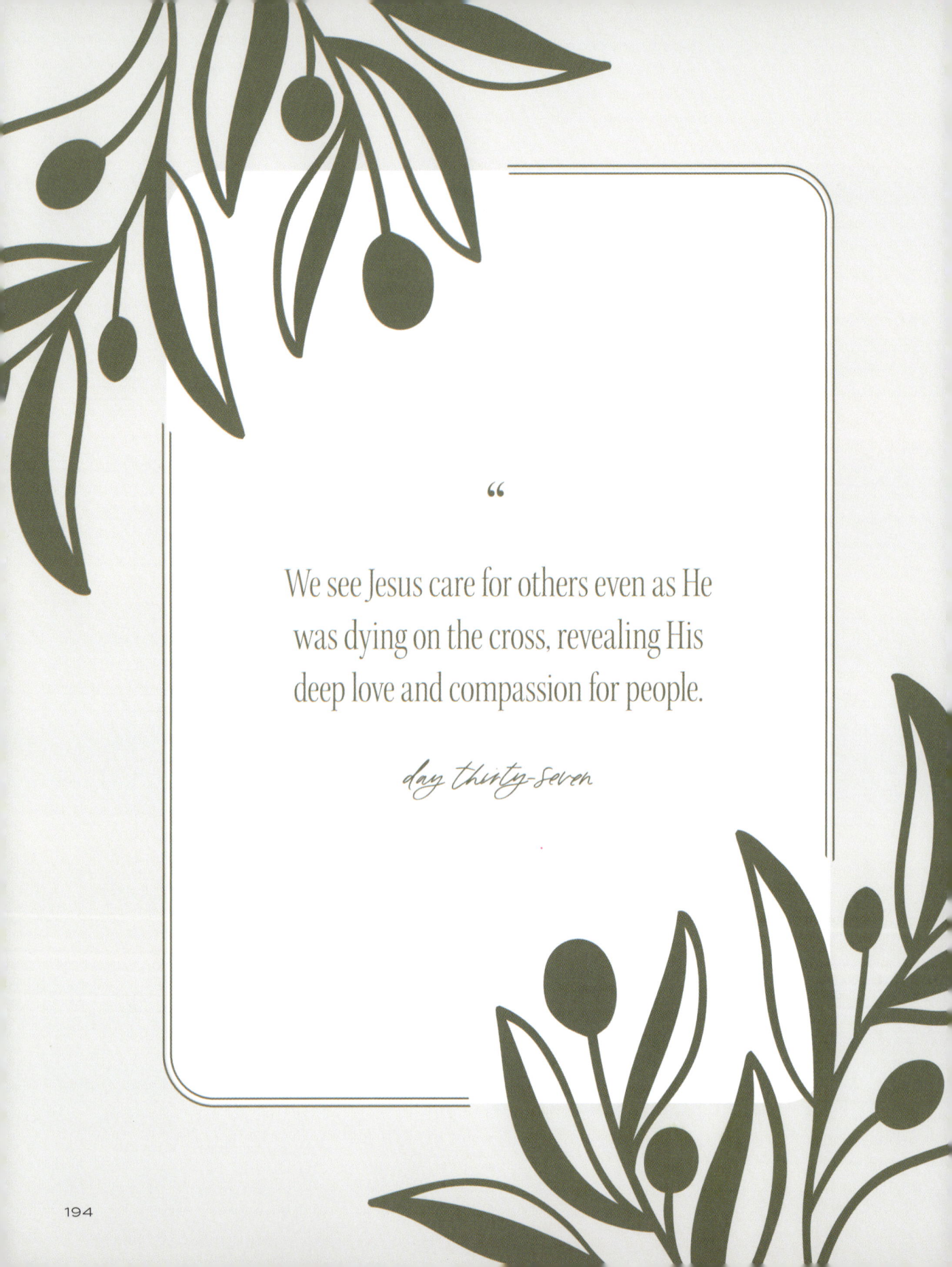

"

We see Jesus care for others even as He was dying on the cross, revealing His deep love and compassion for people.

*day thirty-seven*

# Woman, Here Is Your Son

READ JOHN 19:25–27

When we consider Jesus's ministry, we might think that Jesus was laser-focused on His mission to bring about salvation. But although Jesus remained focused on His mission and what He was called to do, He did not do so at the expense of those around Him. Jesus cared deeply about people, and we see this through the way He talked, healed, and challenged people. In today's verses, we see Jesus care for others even as He was dying on the cross, revealing His deep love and compassion for people.

In reading the Gospels, we do not read many accounts of Jesus interacting with His mother, Mary. We read about Mary before Jesus's birth and when Jesus was little (Luke 1–2). We read about Jesus's interaction with Mary at the wedding of Cana (John 2:1–12). And we read about when Mary and her other children were looking for Jesus (Mark 3:31–32). We can surmise that because Mary knew what Jesus was meant to accomplish (Luke 1:32–33), she supported Him from afar and perhaps attended some of His teachings. But even though we do not know much about what Jesus's relationship was like with Mary, we know that He cared for her deeply, and we can see this at His death on the cross.

Though Jesus is suffering immensely and struggling to breathe on the cross, He takes a moment to provide for His mother. During Jesus's time, it was common for the eldest son to be responsible for his mother, ensuring that she was taken care of physically and financially. While Jesus had other brothers, Jesus wants to ensure that His mother is provided for after His death. So Jesus has His disciple John be the one to take care of Mary, and we see that Mary is brought into John's care for protection and provision.

When Jesus was on the cross, He could have thought only about Himself and what was happening to Him. But Jesus also thought about those around Him, as we read in His prayer of forgiveness and in today's reading with His mother. His actions in John 19 remind us of His selflessness and deep love for others. And although His actions were directed toward Mary, they remind us of what is true for us because of Christ's work on the cross. Through Christ's death and resurrection, we are brought into God's family and will always be taken care of by our heavenly Father.

Jesus loved His mother, even to the very end, and He loved us to the very end as well. Because of His great love, we are forgiven and given a relationship with the One who died and rose again for us. And in response to His great love, we are to love others, showing them the compassion that Christ has shown us.

> "Jesus loved His mother, even to the very end, and He loved us to the very end as well."

## REFLECT

How have you seen God provide and care for you?
What would it look like to reflect Christ's compassion to others?

## PRAY

Thank God for ultimately providing for you by giving you Jesus and forgiving you through Him. Pray that you will live in gratitude for how God has provided for you and that you will show Christ's compassion to others.

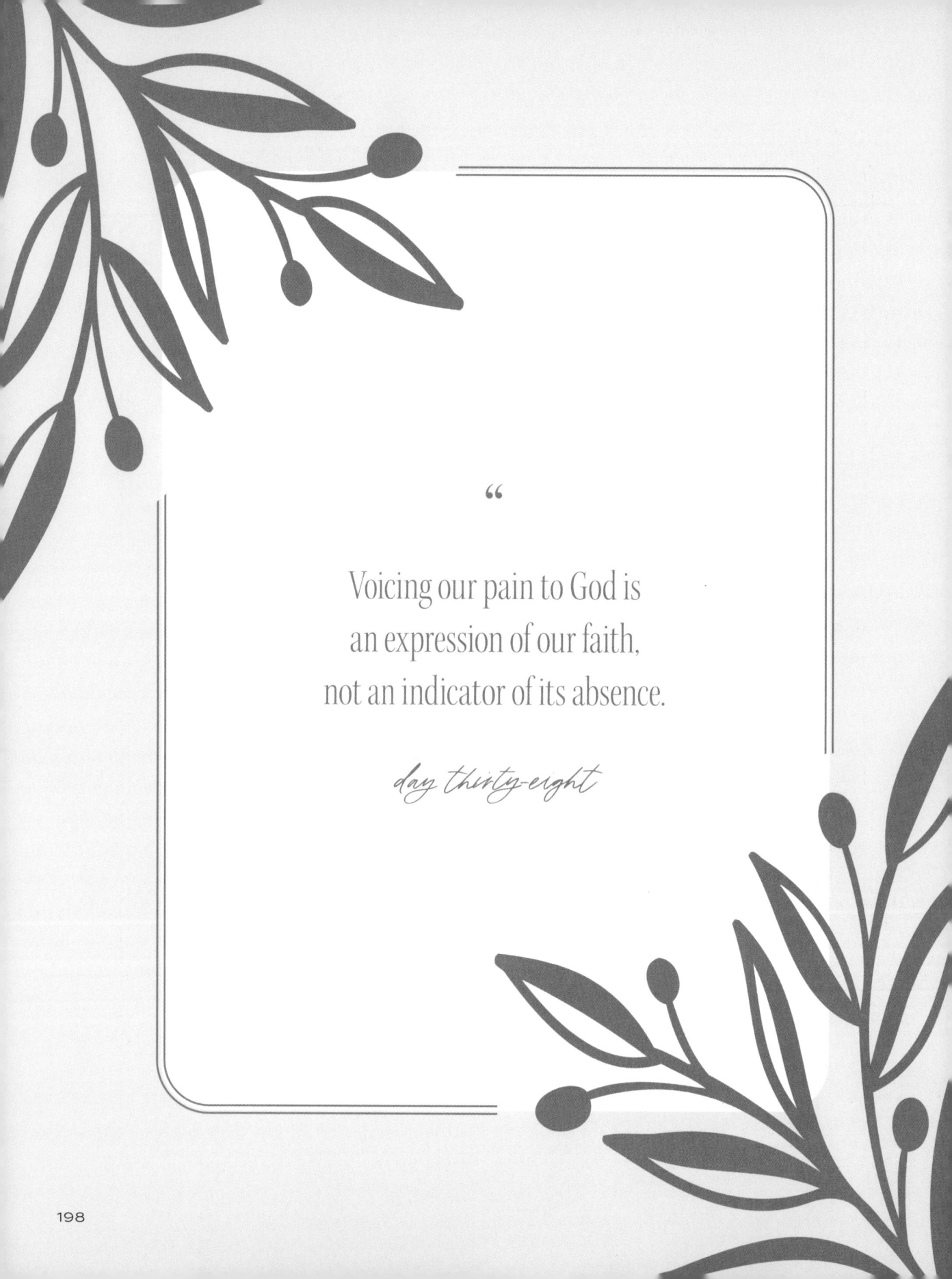

"
Voicing our pain to God is
an expression of our faith,
not an indicator of its absence.

*day thirty-eight*

# Why Have You Abandoned Me?

READ MARK 15:33–34

Life can be hard, and this is something the Bible is quite honest about. In the Psalms, for example, we frequently see God's people complain about how God feels far off, about how they are troubled by fear and anxiety, and about how the wicked seem to prosper while the righteous suffer. The Bible's authors are honest in ways that we might sometimes feel uncomfortable imitating, as if such complaints arise from a lack of faith. But voicing our pain to God is an expression of our faith, not an indicator of its absence.

As Jesus hangs on the cross, darkness begins to cover the land. In the span of a few hours, Jesus has been flogged, mocked, unjustly accused, and abandoned by His disciples. And now, He is on a cross, enduring physical agony. Worse, though, is the darkness and what it represents: the judgment of God that is falling on Jesus, who is dying in place of sinners (Exodus 10:22, Amos 8:9–10).

And thus Jesus cries out, "My God, my God, why have you abandoned me?" (Mark 15:34).

Jesus is quoting the opening words of Psalm 22, which was composed by David. While we do not know David's specific circumstances when he wrote this psalm, he was clearly suffering. He felt abandoned by God and that his prayers were not being heard (Psalm 22:1–2). He is despised and mocked by others (verses 6–7). People assumed that if God were pleased with David, He would rescue him (verse 8). His strength was gone (verse 15), and he was all alone (verse 11). Many of the details of this psalm quite closely fit Jesus's circumstances, which may be why He chooses to quote it.

But there is much more to Psalm 22 than despair. For David to even voice his concerns to God is an indicator that David believes his concerns matter to God. And this belief was well-founded because in verse 22, the psalm's tone pivots. Though beginning in pain, the psalm closes on a note of victory, of vindication. God has heard David's prayers and intervened in his sufferings (verses 22–31).

Jesus quotes a psalm that begins in pain but ends in victory. He knows this will mirror His own trajectory, for not only has He prophesied His suffering and death several times up to this point, but He has also prophesied His resurrection (Mark 8:31, 9:31, 10:33–34). And this will be our own path as His followers (Mark 8:34–35). On that path, we are invited to voice our own pain to God. In doing so, we not only express our faith that our concerns are seen by and matter to Him, but we also remind ourselves that our pain will one day cease, and we will live in God's presence forever.

> "Jesus quotes a psalm that begins in pain but ends in victory."

**REFLECT**

Do you ever feel abandoned by God? Do you ever feel that He has forgotten you or hidden His face from you (see Psalm 13:1)? What encouragement can Psalm 22 and Mark 15:34 offer to us in these moments?

**PRAY**

Ask that in the midst of difficult circumstances, you would be reminded that God hears your cries, is concerned about you, and that He is committed to your good.

"

Even in His dying moments, Jesus is fulfilling Scripture. His presence on the cross is not a deviation from God's purposes but the fulfillment of them.

*day thirty-nine*

# I'm Thirsty; It Is Finished

READ JOHN 19:28-30

We make many plans over the course of our lives. Sometimes, our plans are carried out to perfection. But for other plans, there comes a moment when we realize that something has gone wrong. For many of the onlookers present at Jesus's crucifixion, it probably seemed as though Jesus's plans had gone horribly wrong. Yet the Bible reminds us that even here, hanging on a cross, Jesus is in full control of what is happening to Him.

In the span of three quick verses, we come to the fifth and sixth of Jesus's sayings from the cross. The first, "I'm thirsty" (verse 28), would be a natural thing for someone hanging on a cross to say. Jesus has, after all, been severely tortured and has been hanging on the cross in the sunlight for hours.

But more seems to be going on here, because John indicates that Jesus says this not only because He is physically thirsty (though that is probably true); He says it so "that the Scripture might be fulfilled." What Scripture does this request fulfill, though? Some believe it to be a reference to Psalm 22:15, which John quotes just a few verses earlier (John 19:24). More likely, though, Jesus is referencing Psalm 69:21 ("for my thirst they gave me vinegar to drink"), because in response to Jesus's words, the soldiers offer him "wine vinegar" (John 19:29, NIV). Even in His dying moments, Jesus is fulfilling Scripture. His presence on the cross is not a deviation from God's purposes but the fulfillment of them.

Then, after Jesus receives the sour wine, He says, "It is finished" (John 19:30). Jesus has fully carried out the work given to Him by God and glorified Him in the process (see John 17:4). When we compare this moment to Matthew 27:48–50 and Mark 15:36–37, it seems as though these words were shouted. This final shout of Jesus's was not one of agony but of victory.

Even here, as His life expires, we see Jesus in control. Earlier in John's Gospel, Jesus said that He lays down His life "of [His] own accord" (John 10:18, NIV). And here John likewise describes the moment of Jesus's death as a voluntary act: "he gave up his spirit." This has always been the plan: to lay down His life to take away the sins of the world (John 1:29, 10:11). Because the plan has been carried out, "it is finished." And because it is finished, we "will not perish but have eternal life" (John 3:16).

"This final shout of Jesus's was not one of agony, but of victory."

**REFLECT**

When we sin, we can sometimes feel as though we have to do something as payment to God—that we must work off a sin debt to Him. How do Jesus's words, "It is finished" comfort us in these moments?

**PRAY**

Give thanks to God for creating and perfectly carrying out His plan to bring salvation to sinners. Spend time thanking Him for the incredible love He has shown to you.

> In the face of unimaginable suffering, Jesus continued to entrust Himself to the Father.

*day forty*

# Into Your Hands I Entrust My Spirit

READ LUKE 23:46

Suffering has a way of forcing us to confront what we truly believe about God. It can be a catalyst for us to draw close to Him, knowing that He is with us in the midst of the pain. It can tempt us to become angry with Him and heed the advice of Job's wife to "Curse God and die" in response to our suffering (Job 2:9). As Jesus hung on the cross, though, He took the former approach. In the face of unimaginable suffering, Jesus continued to entrust Himself to the Father.

Today we come to the seventh and final of Jesus's sayings from the cross, recorded for us in Luke 23:46: "Father, into your hands I entrust my spirit." Like other sayings we have considered in the previous two days, Jesus is again quoting words from the Psalms—in this case, Psalm 31, which is a plea from David for God to deliver him from powerful enemies.

As with Jesus's quotation of Psalm 22 (Day 38), it is important to keep the entire psalm in view, not just the particular portion Jesus cites. Though Psalm 31 is a psalm of anguish and desperation, it is also one of confident trust in God. David calls God his "refuge" and his "fortress" (Psalm 31:1, 3). And immediately after David says, "Into your hand I entrust my spirit," he writes, "you have redeemed me, Lord, God of truth" (Psalm 31:5). Like David, Jesus—in quoting these words—entrusts Himself to God's care and then He "breathed his last" (Luke 23:46). To His final breath, Jesus draws close to the Father.

In this context, Luke records, "The curtain of the sanctuary was split down the middle" (Luke 23:45). Given that the curtain prevented anyone from entering the innermost part of the sanctuary where God's presence was, this is a significant act. It demonstrates that because of Jesus's death, we now have access to the presence of God. Whereas "the way into the most holy place had not yet been disclosed" in the past, Jesus's death brings us beyond the curtain to God's presence (Hebrews 9:8, 10:19–20).

And this makes all the difference in how we respond to suffering in our own lives. For example, as Stephen is being stoned to death in Acts 7, he looks up to heaven and sees the risen Jesus. And echoing Jesus's own words, he cries, "Lord Jesus, receive my spirit" (Acts 7:59). Hebrews 12:1–3 likewise implores us to persevere in suffering by looking to Jesus who for "the joy that lay before him . . . endured the cross . . . and sat down at the right hand of the throne of God."

Jesus suffered before He was glorified. And that is our path as well. Knowing this, we too in our suffering can continue to entrust ourselves to God, knowing that He will ultimately rescue us from all our troubles.

> "To His final breath, Jesus draws close to the Father."

## REFLECT

When faced with suffering, what is your response to God?
Do you entrust yourself to Him? Get angry at Him? Ignore Him?
How can Jesus's response to suffering encourage you in your own suffering?

## PRAY

Pray that God would help you to endure suffering
by entrusting yourself to Him.

## week 7 conclusion

In Romans 8:32, Paul writes: "[God] did not even spare his own Son but gave him up for us all. How will he not also with him grant us everything?"

God gave what was most precious to Him—His Son, Jesus—for us. He spared no expense for our good. This truth is likewise communicated in what is perhaps one of the Bible's most recognized verses: "For God loved the world in this way: He gave his one and only Son, so that everyone who believes in him will not perish but have eternal life" (John 3:16). We have seen that love on full display this week. Jesus willingly endured the judgment our sins deserved so that we would not have to. Because of His love and His sacrifice, we can now have eternal life. Spend time thanking God for these incredible truths!

> God gave what was most precious to Him —
> His Son, Jesus — for us.
> He spared no expense for our good.

> This study has been an exploration of what "Jesus began to do and teach."

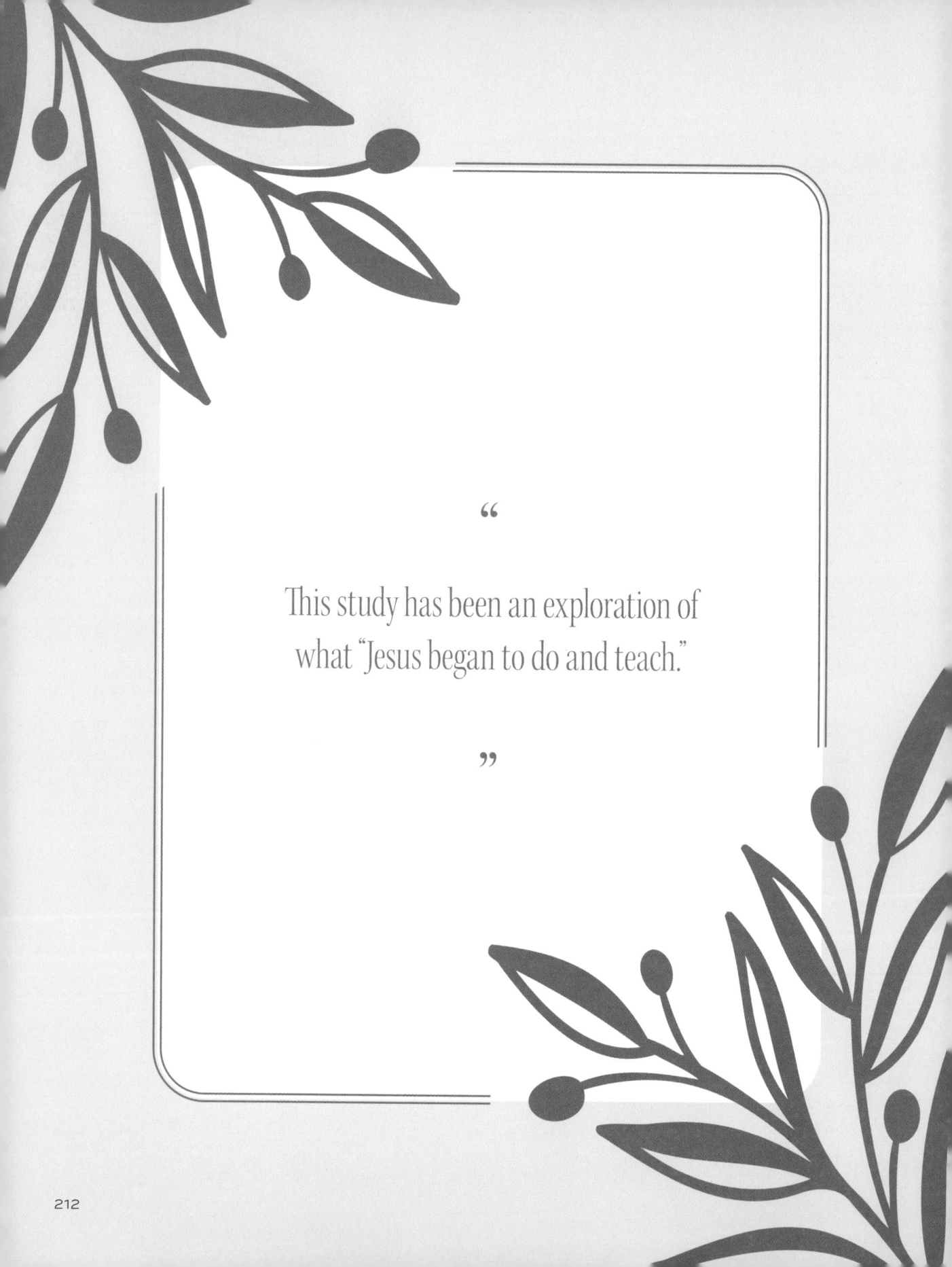

# Conclusion — You Will Be My Witnesses

READ ACTS 1:1–11

Sometime after Luke wrote his Gospel, he wrote a follow-up volume, the book of Acts. It begins with a passive reference by Luke to his "first narrative" and calls it a record of "all that Jesus began to do and teach until the day he was taken up" (Acts 1:1–2).

This study has been an exploration of what "Jesus began to do and teach." We have seen Jesus's declaration that God's kingdom "has come near" and that people should, therefore, "Repent and believe the good news" (Mark 1:15). We have considered what Jesus's seven "I Am" statements tell us about who He is. We have seen Jesus's heart for people on the margins. We have listened to Him teach about God's love for us and how we are to treat others. And in the final two weeks, we have dwelt on Jesus's sufferings and His final words from the cross.

But Luke's comment in Acts 1:1–2 is also a bit curious. After all, his Gospel covered quite a bit of ground. It covered Jesus's miraculous conception in Mary's womb, as well as His birth. Luke then covered a great deal of Jesus's ministry before describing His death, resurrection, and ascension to heaven. Such a comprehensive account of Jesus's life might lead us to expect Luke to refer to his Gospel as a record of *all that Jesus did and taught*. But that is not what he says. Instead, it is a record of what Jesus "began to do and teach" (Acts 1:1).

The implication of that word "began" is that Jesus is *still* at work, even after His ascension to heaven. The next few verses in Acts explain how Jesus can still be at work in the world even while He is in heaven. In Acts 1:4, he tells His disciples to stay in Jerusalem and wait for the promised Holy Spirit. Then in verse 8, He describes the effect of the Spirit's arrival: "you will receive power when the Holy Spirit has come on you, and you will be my witnesses in Jerusalem, in all Judea and Samaria, and to the ends of the earth." In the words of F.F. Bruce, the book of Acts records how Jesus continued to work and teach, "no longer in visible presence on earth but by his Spirit in his followers" (Bruce, 30).

As Christians, we have been given the Holy Spirit. And through His Spirit-empowered people, Jesus continues to work in the world today. What we have seen Him do and teach throughout this study, He continues to do through us as we follow Him and live out His teachings. Let us then pay close attention to what Scripture shows us about Jesus, and let us pray that we might faithfully represent Him and be His witnesses to others in our own lives.

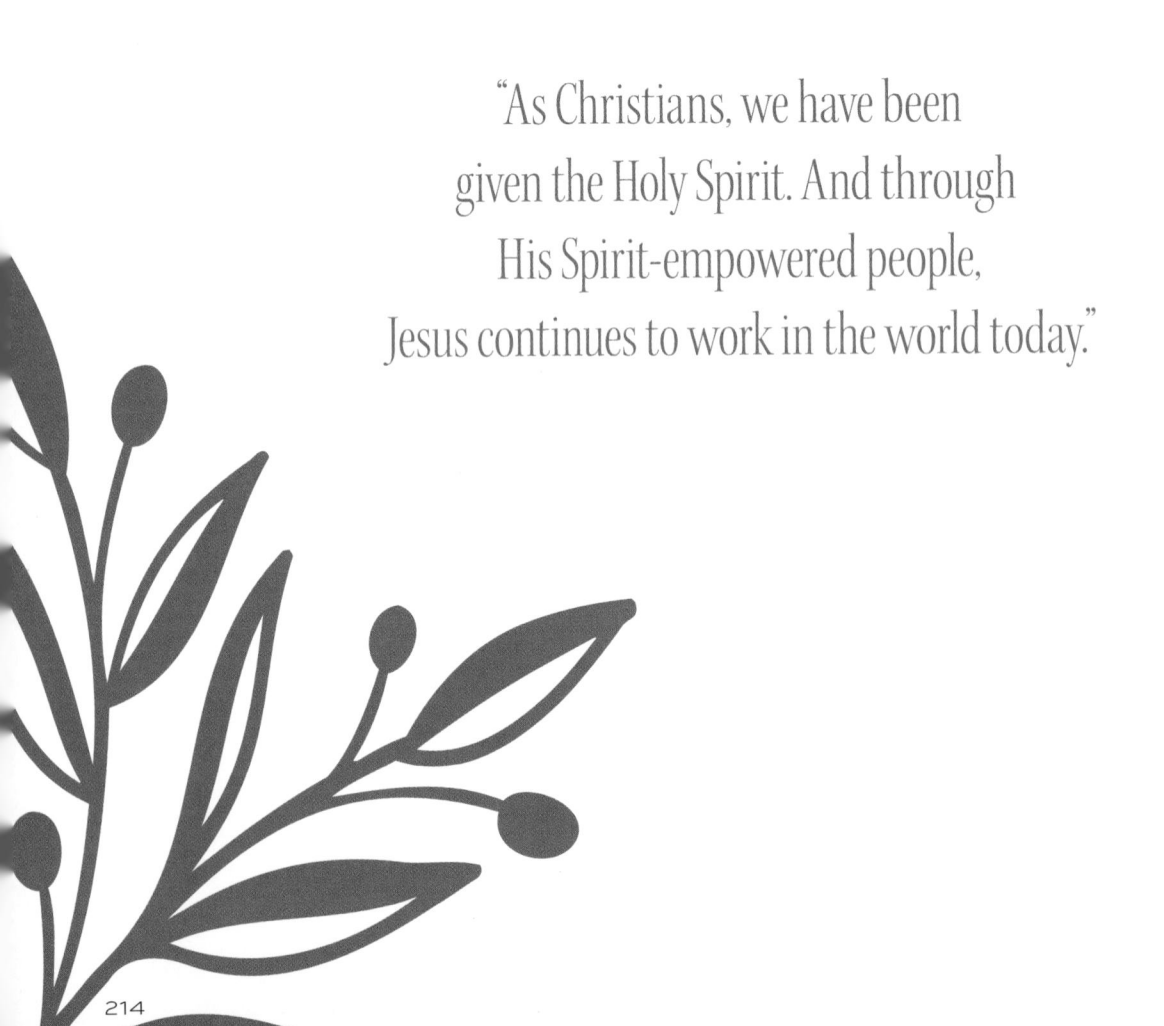

> "As Christians, we have been given the Holy Spirit. And through His Spirit-empowered people, Jesus continues to work in the world today."

**REFLECT**

What have been some of your biggest takeaways from this study? How is God calling you to respond to what He has shown you in these past few weeks?

**PRAY**

Ask for God to help you be a faithful representation of Jesus to those around you. Pray that others would love Jesus more as you model His love to them.

# What is *the* Gospel?

*Thank you for reading and enjoying this study with us! We are abundantly grateful for the Word of God, the instruction we glean from it, and the ever-growing understanding it provides for us of God's character. We are also thankful that Scripture continually points to one thing in innumerable ways: the gospel.*

We remember our brokenness when we read about the fall of Adam and Eve in the garden of Eden (Genesis 3), where sin entered into a perfect world and maimed it. We remember the necessity that something innocent must die to pay for our sin when we read about the atoning sacrifices in the Old Testament. We read that we have all sinned and fallen short of the glory of God (Romans 3:23) and that the penalty for our brokenness, the wages of our sin, is death (Romans 6:23). We all need grace and mercy, but most importantly, we all need a Savior.

We consider the goodness of God when we realize that He did not plan to leave us in this dire state. We see His promise to buy us back from the clutches of sin and death in Genesis 3:15. And we see that promise accomplished with Jesus Christ on the cross. Jesus Christ knew no sin yet became sin so that we might become righteous through His sacrifice (2 Corinthians 5:21). Jesus was tempted in every way that we are and lived sinlessly. He was reviled yet still yielded Himself for our sake, that we may have life abundant in Him. Jesus lived the perfect life that we could not live and died the death that we deserved.

The gospel is profound yet simple. There are many mysteries in it that we will never understand this side of heaven, but there is still overwhelming weight to its implications in this life. The gospel tells of our sinfulness and God's goodness and a gracious gift that compels a response. We are saved by grace through faith, which means that we rest with faith in the grace that Jesus Christ displayed on the cross (Ephesians 2:8–9). We cannot save ourselves from our brokenness or do any amount of good works to merit God's favor. Still, we can have faith that what Jesus accomplished in His death, burial, and resurrection was more than enough for our salvation and our eternal delight. When we accept God, we are commanded to die to ourselves and our sinful desires and live a life worthy of the calling we have received (Ephesians 4:1). The gospel compels us to be sanctified, and in so doing, we are conformed to the likeness of Christ Himself. This is hope. This is redemption. This is the gospel.

**GENESIS 3:15**

*I will put hostility between you and the woman, and between your offspring and her offspring. He will strike your head, and you will strike his heel.*

**ROMANS 3:23**

*For all have sinned and fall short of the glory of God.*

**ROMANS 6:23**

*For the wages of sin is death, but the gift of God is eternal life in Christ Jesus our Lord.*

**2 CORINTHIANS 5:21**

*He made the one who did not know sin to be sin for us, so that in him we might become the righteousness of God.*

**EPHESIANS 2:8-9**

*For you are saved by grace through faith, and this is not from yourselves; it is God's gift—not from works, so that no one can boast.*

**EPHESIANS 4:1-3**

*Therefore I, the prisoner in the Lord, urge you to walk worthy of the calling you have received, with all humility and gentleness, with patience, bearing with one another in love, making every effort to keep the unity of the Spirit through the bond of peace.*

## BIBLIOGRAPHY

Bock, Darrell L. *Luke*. The NIV Application Commentary. Grand Rapids: Zondervan, 1996.

Bruce, F.F. *The Book of the Acts: Revised Edition*. The New International Commentary on the New Testament. Grand Rapids: Wm. B. Eerdmans Publishing Company, 1992.

Bunyan, John. *The Pilgrim's Progress In Modern English*. Revised and Updated by L. Edward Hazelbaker. Gainesville, FL: Bridge-Logos, 1998.

Carson, D.A. *The Gospel According to John*. The Pillar New Testament Commentary. Grand Rapids: Wm. B. Eerdmans Publishing Company, 1991.

Chen, Diane G. *Luke*. New Covenant Commentary Series. Eugene, OR: Cascade Books, 2017.

Coleman, Aubrey, Kyra Daniels, Miranda Mae Ewing, Alexa Hess, and Kristyn Perez. *40 Days with Jesus: A Study on the Life of Christ*. Spring, Texas. The Daily Grace Co., 2021.

Edwards, James R. *The Gospel According to Mark*, The Pillar New Testament Commentary. Grand Rapids, MI; Leicester, England: Eerdmans; Apollos, 2002.

Ferguson, Sinclair B. *Let's Study Mark*. Carlisle, PA: The Banner of Truth Trust, 1999.

Green, Michael. *The Message of Matthew*. The Bible Speaks Today. Downers Grove: InterVarsity Press, 2000.

Lane, William L. *The Gospel of Mark*. The New International Commentary on the New Testament. Grand Rapids: Wm. B. Eerdmans Publishing Co., 1974.

Milne, Bruce. *The Message of John*. The Bible Speaks Today. Downers Grove: InterVarsity Press, 1993.

Morris, Leon. *The Gospel According to John* (Revised). The New International Commentary on the New Testament. Grand Rapids: Wm. B. Eerdmans Publishing Co., 1995.

Morris, Leon. *The Gospel According to Matthew*. The Pillar New Testament Commentary. Grand Rapids, MI; Leicester, England: W.B. Eerdmans; Inter-Varsity Press, 1992.

Morris, Leon. *Luke: An Introduction and Commentary*, vol. 3, Tyndale New Testament Commentaries. Downers Grove, IL: InterVarsity Press, 1988.

Mounce, Robert H. *Matthew*. New International Biblical Commentary. Peabody, MA: Hendrickson Publishers, Inc., 1991.

Reiner, Rob, dir. *The Princess Bride*. 20th Century Fox, 1987.

Robinson, Robert. "Come, Thou Fount of Every Blessing." In *A Teaching Hymnal*. Edited by Clayton J. Schmit. 132. Eugene, OR: Cascade Books, 2018. https://hymnary.org/text/come_thou_fount_of_every_blessing.

Schnabel, Eckhard J. *Mark*. Tyndale New Testament Commentaries. Downers Grove: InterVarsity Press, 2017.

Stott, John R.W. *The Message of Acts*. The Bible Speaks Today. Downers Grove: InterVarsity Press, 1990.

Webber, Robert E. *Ancient-Future Time: Forming Spirituality through the Christian Year*. Grand Rapids: Baker Books, 2004.

*The Westminster Standards*. Suwanee, GA: Great Commission Publications, 2007.

Witherington, Ben III. *The Gospel of Mark: A Socio-Rhetorical Commentary*. Grand Rapids: Wm. B. Eerdmans Publishing Co., 2001.

*Thank you for studying God's Word with us!*

### CONNECT WITH US
@thedailygraceco
@dailygracepodcast

### CONTACT US
info@thedailygraceco.com

### SHARE
#thedailygraceco

### VISIT US ONLINE
www.thedailygraceco.com

### MORE DAILY GRACE
Daily Grace® Podcast